DK EYEWITNESS TRAVEL
15-MINUTE
SPANISH

D0488391

DK EYEWITNESS TRAVEL

15-MINUTE
SPANISH

LEARN SPANISH
IN JUST 15
MINUTES A DAY

ANA BREMÓN

DORLING KINDERSLEY

London, New York, Munich, Melbourne,
and Delhi

Dorling Kindersley Limited
Senior Editor Angeles Gavira
Project Art Editor Vanessa Marr
DTP Designer John Goldsmid
Production Controller Luca Frassinetti
Publishing Manager Liz Wheeler
Managing Art Editor Philip Ormerod
Publishing Director Jonathan Metcalf
Art Director Bryn Walls

Language content for Dorling Kindersley by
g-and-w publishing

Produced for Dorling Kindersley by
Schermuly Design Co.
Art Editor Hugh Schermuly
Project Editor Cathy Meeus
Special photography Mike Good

First published in Great Britain in 2005 by
Dorling Kindersley Limited
80 Strand, London WC2R 0RL
A Penguin Company
Copyright © 2005 Dorling Kindersley Limited

10 9

15-Minute Spanish is also available in a pack
with two CDs
ISBN-13: 978 1 4053 0973 8

Colour reproduction by Colourscan, Singapore
Printed and bound in China by Leo Paper
Products Limited

See our complete catalogue at
www.dk.com

Contents

How to use this book

This main part of the book is devoted to 12 themed
chapters, broken down into five 15-minute daily lessons,
the last of which is a revision lesson. So, in just 12 weeks
you will have completed the course. A concluding
reference section contains a menu guide and English-to-
Spanish and Spanish-to-English dictionaries.

Warm up and clock
Each day starts with a one-minute warm-up that
encourages you to recall vocabulary or phrases
you have learned previously. A clock to the right
of the heading bar indicates the amount of time
you are expected to spend on each exercise.

Instructions
Each exercise is numbered and introduced by
instructions that explain what to do. In some
cases additional information is given about the
language point being covered.

Cultural/Conversational tip
These panels provide additional
insights into life in Spain and
language usage.

Text styles
Distinctive text
styles differentiate
Spanish and
English, and the
pronunciation
guide (see right).

In conversation
Illustrated dialogues
reflecting how
vocabulary and
phrases are used in
everyday situations
appear throughout
the book.

How to use the flap
The book's cover flaps
allow you to conceal
the Spanish so that
you can test whether
you have remembered
correctly.

Revision pages
A recap of selected
elements of previous
lessons helps to
reinforce your
knowledge.

Useful phrases
Selected phrases
relevant to the topic
help you speak and
understand.

Pronunciation guide

This book teaches European Spanish, which
differs in pronunciation from the various
dialects spoken in Latin America. A few
Spanish sounds require special explanation:

c	a Spanish **c** is pronounced *th* before **i** or **e** but **k** before other vowels: **cinco** <u>theenkoh</u> (*five*)
h	**h** is always silent: **hola** o-lah (*hello*)
j (g)	a Spanish **j** (and **g** before **i** or **e**) is pronounced as a strong *h*, as if saying <u>h</u>at emphazing the first letter
ll	pronounced *y* as in <u>yes</u>
ñ	pronounced *ny* like the sound in *can<u>y</u>on*
r	a Spanish **r** is trilled like a Scottish **r**, especially at the beginning of a word and when doubled
v	a Spanish **v** is halfway between an English *b* and *v*
z	a Spanish **z** is pronounced *th*

Spanish vowels tend to be pronounced
shorter than their English equivalents:

a	as the English *father*
e	as the English *wet*
i	as the English *keep*
o	as the English *boat*
u	as the English *boot*

After each word or phrase you will find a
pronunciation transcription, with underlining
showing the stress. Remember that this can
only be an approximation; there is no
substitute for listening to and mimicking
native speakers.

Say it
In these exercises you
are asked to apply
what you have learned
using different
vocabulary.

5 Say It

Do you have a single
room, please?

For six nights.

Is breakfast included?

Menu guide
Use this guide as a
reference for food
terminology and
popular Spanish
dishes.

Dictionary
A mini-dictionary
provides ready
reference from
English to Spanish
and Spanish to
English for 2,500
words.

1 Warm up

The Warm Up appears at the beginning of each lesson. It will remind you of what you have already learned and prepare you for moving ahead with the new subject.

Hola
Hello

In Spain women often greet with one or two kisses on the cheek and men shake other men's hands, although men may kiss or embrace younger male relatives or close friends. In more formal situations – among strangers or in a business context – a handshake is the norm.

¡Hola!
o-lah
Hello!

2 Words to remember

Look at these greetings and say them aloud. Conceal the text on the left with the cover flap and try to remember the Spanish for each item. Check your answers.

Buenos días. bwenos deeyas	*Good morning/day.*
Me llamo Ana. may yamoh anna	*My name is Ana.*
Encantado/-a. enkan-tadoh/-ah	*Pleased to meet you (man/woman speaking).*
Buenas tardes (noches). bwenas tardes (noches)	*Good afternoon/ evening (night).*

Cultural tip The Spanish frequently address people as "señor" (sir), "señora" (madam, for older women), and "señorita" (miss, for young women). With first names use "Don" for men or "Doña" for women: Don Juan, Doña Ana.

3 In conversation: formal

Buenos días. Me llamo Concha García.
bwenos deeyas. may yamoh konchah garthee-ah

Good day. My name's Concha García.

Señor López, encantado.
senyor lopeth, enkan-tadoh

Mr López, pleased to meet you.

Encantada.
enkan-tadah

Pleased to meet you.

4 Put into practice

Join in this conversation. Read the Spanish beside the pictures on the left and then follow the instructions to make your reply. Then test yourself by concealing the answers on the right with the cover flap.

Buenas tardes señor.
bwenas tardes senyor
Good evening, sir.

Say: Good evening,
madam.

Buenas tardes señora.
bwenas tardes
senyorah

Me llamo Julia.
may yamoh hoolya
My name is Julia.

Say. Pleased to meet
you.

Encantado.
enkan-tadoh

5 Useful phrases

Read these phrases aloud several times and try to memorize them. Conceal the Spanish with the cover flap and test yourself.

What's your name?	**¿Cómo se llama?** komo seh yamah
Goodbye.	**Adiós.** addy-os
Thank you.	**Gracias.** grathyas
See you soon/ tomorrow.	**Hasta pronto/mañana.** astah prontoh/ manyanah

6 In conversation: informal

Entonces, ¿hasta mañana?
entonthes, astah manyanah

So, see you tomorrow?

Sí, adiós.
see, addy-os

Yes, goodbye.

Adiós. Hasta pronto.
addy-os. astah prontoh

Goodbye. See you soon.

Las relaciones
Relatives

1 Warm up

Say "hello" and "goodbye" in Spanish. (pp.8–9)

Now say "My name is…". (pp.8–9)

Say "sir" and "madam". (pp.8–9)

The Spanish equivalents of *mum* and *dad* are **mamá** and **papá**. The male plural can refer to both sexes, for example – **niños** (*boys* and *children*), **padres** (*fathers* and *parents*), **abuelos** (*grandfathers* and *grandparents*), **tíos** (*uncles* and *aunt and uncle*), **hermanos** (*brothers* and *siblings*), and so on.

2 Match and repeat

Look at the people in this scene and match their numbers with the list at the side. Read the Spanish words aloud. Now, conceal the list with the cover flap and test yourself.

1 **la hermana**
 lah air**man**ah

2 **el abuelo**
 el a**bwe**loh

3 **el padre**
 el **pah**dray

4 **el hermano**
 el air**man**oh

5 **la abuela**
 lah a**bwe**lah

6 **la hija**
 lah **ee**-hah

7 **la madre**
 lah **mah**dray

8 **el hijo**
 el **ee**-hoh

❶ sister
❷ grandfather
❸ father
❹ brother
❻ daughter
❺ grandmother
❼ mother
❽ son

Conversational tip In Spanish, things as well as people are masculine or feminine – for example, "wine" is masculine ("el vino") but "milk" is feminine ("la leche"). Use "los" and "las" for masculine and feminine plurals, respectively. For "a/an", use "un" for masculine and "una" for feminine items.

3 Words to remember: relatives

Familiarize yourself with these words. Read them aloud several times and try to memorize them. Conceal the Spanish with the cover flap and test yourself.

el marido
el mareedoh
husband

la mujer
lah moo-hair
wife

Estoy casado/-a.
estoy kasadoh/-ah
I'm married (m/f).

father/mother-in-law	**el suegro/la suegra** el swegroh/lah swegrah
stepfather	**el padrastro** el padras-troh
stepmother	**la madrastra** lah madras-trah
children (male/female)	**los niños/las niñas** los neenyos/las neenyas
uncle/aunt	**el tío/la tía** lah tee-ah/el tee-oh
cousin	**el primo/la prima** el preemoh/lah preemah
I have four children.	**Tengo cuatro niños.** tengoh kwatroh neenyos
I have two stepdaughters and a stepson.	**Tengo dos hijastras y un hijastro.** tengoh dos ee-hastras ee oon ee-hastroh

4 Words to remember: numbers

Memorize these words and then test yourself using the cover flap.

Careful when you use the number one. When you use **uno** in front of a word it changes to **un** or **una**, depending on whether that word is masculine or feminine. For example: **Tengo un hijo** (*I have one son*), **Tengo una hija** (*I have one daughter*).

one	**uno/-a** oonoh/-ah
two	**dos** dos
three	**tres** tres
four	**cuatro** kwatroh
five	**cinco** theenkoh
six	**seis** seys
seven	**siete** syetay
eight	**ocho** ochoh
nine	**nueve** nwebay
ten	**diez** dyeth

5 Say it

I have five sons.

I have three sisters and a brother.

I have two children.

Say the Spanish for as many members of the family as you can. (pp.10–11)

Say "I have two sons". (pp.10–11)

Mi familia
My family

There are two ways of saying *you* in Spanish, **usted** for formal situations and **tú** in informal ones. There is also a formal way of saying *your* – **su** (singular) and **sus** (plural): **usted y su mujer** (*you and your wife*), **¿Son ésos sus hijos?** (*Are those your sons?*). **Su** and **sus** also mean *his* and *her*.

2 Words to remember

Say these words aloud a few times. Conceal the Spanish with the cover flap and try to remember the Spanish word for each item.

mi mee	*my (with singular)*
mis mees	*my (with plural)*
tu too	*your (informal with singular)*
tus toos	*your (informal with plural)*
su soo	*your (formal with singular)*
sus soos	*your (formal with plural)*
su soo	*his/her (with singular) their (with singular)*
sus soos	*his/her (with plural) their (with plural)*

Éstos son mis padres.
estos son mees pahdres
These are my parents.

3 In conversation

¿Tiene usted niños?
tyenay oosted neenyos

Do you have any children?

Sí, tengo dos hijas.
see, tengoh dos ee-has

Yes, I have two daughters.

Éstas son mis hijas. ¿Y usted?
estas son mees ee-has. ee oosted

These are my daughters. And you?

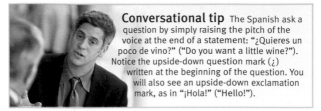

Conversational tip The Spanish ask a question by simply raising the pitch of the voice at the end of a statement: "¿Quieres un poco de vino?" ("Do you want a little wine?"). Notice the upside-down question mark (¿) written at the beginning of the question. You will also see an upside-down exclamation mark, as in "¡Hola!" ("Hello!").

4 Useful phrases

Read these phrases aloud several times and try to memorize them. Conceal the Spanish with the cover flap and test yourself.

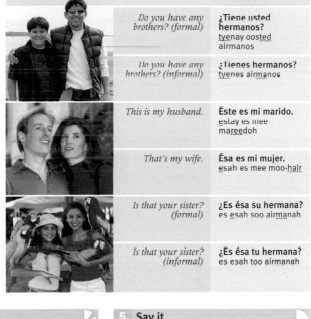

Do you have any brothers? (formal)	**¿Tiene usted hermanos?** tyenay oosted airmanos	
Do you have any brothers? (informal)	**¿Tienes hermanos?** tyenes airmanos	
This is my husband.	**Éste es mi marido.** estay es mee mareedoh	
That's my wife.	**Ésa es mi mujer.** esah es mee moo-hair	
Is that your sister? (formal)	**¿Es ésa su hermana?** es esah soo airmanah	
Is that your sister? (informal)	**¿Es ésa tu hermana?** es esah too airmanah	

No, pero tengo un hijastro.
noh, peroh tengoh oon ee-hastroh

No, but I have a stepson.

5 Say it

Do you have any brothers and sisters? (formal)

Do you have any children? (informal)

I have two sisters.

This is my wife, María.

1 Warm up

Say "See you soon". (pp.8–9)

Say "I am married" (pp.10–11) and "I have a wife". (pp.12–13)

Ser y tener
To be and to have

Two of the most important verbs are **ser** (*to be*) and **tener** (*to have*). Note that there are different ways of saying *you*, *we*, and *they*, with formal and informal, singular and plural, and masculine and feminine forms. Pronouns (*I*, *you*, etc.) are omitted where the sense is clear.

2 Ser: to be

Familiarize yourself with **ser** (*to be*). When you are confident, practise the sample sentences below. Note: there is another verb meaning "to be" – **estar**, which is discussed on page 49.

yo soy yoh soy	*I am*
tú eres too <u>eh</u>-res	*you are (informal singular)*
usted es oos<u>ted</u> es	*you are (formal singular)*
él/ella es el/<u>eh</u>-yah es	*he/she is*
nosotros/-as somos no<u>sot</u>ros/-as <u>som</u>os	*we are (masculine/feminine)*
vosotros/-as sois bo<u>sot</u>ros/-as soys	*you are (informal plural, m/f)*
ustedes son oos<u>ted</u>es son	*you are (formal plural)*
ellos/-as son <u>eh</u>-yos/-yas son	*they are (masculine/feminine)*

Yo soy inglesa.
yoh soy eeng<u>les</u>ah
I'm English.

¿De dónde es usted? day <u>don</u>day es oos<u>ted</u>	*Where are you from?*
Es mi hermana. es mee air<u>man</u>ah	*She is my sister.*
Somos españoles. <u>som</u>os espan<u>yol</u>es	*We're Spanish.*

3 Tener: to have

Practise **tener** (*to have*) and the sample sentences, then test yourself.

I have	**yo tengo** yoh <u>ten</u>goh
you have *(informal singular)*	**tú tienes** too <u>tye</u>nes
you have *(formal singular)*	**usted tiene** oosted <u>tye</u>nay
he/she has	**él/ella tiene** el/<u>eh</u>-yah <u>tye</u>nay
we have *(masculine/feminine)*	**nosotros/-as tenemos** no<u>so</u>tros/-as te<u>nay</u>mos
you have *(informal plural, m/f)*	**vosotros/-as teneis** bo<u>so</u>tros/-as te<u>nays</u>
you have *(formal plural)*	**ustedes tienen** oos<u>te</u>des <u>tye</u>nen
they have *(masculine/feminine)*	**ellos/-as tienen** eh-yos/-yas <u>tye</u>nen

¿Tiene rosas rojas?
<u>tye</u>nay <u>ro</u>sas <u>ro</u>has
Do you have red roses?

He has a meeting.	**Tiene una reunión.** <u>tye</u>nay <u>oo</u>nah re-<u>oo</u>nyon
Do you have a mobile phone?	**¿Tiene usted móvil?** <u>tye</u>nay oos<u>ted</u> <u>mob</u>eel?
How many brothers and sisters do you have?	**¿Cuántos hermanos tiene usted?** <u>kwan</u>tos air<u>ma</u>nos <u>tye</u>nay oos<u>ted</u>

4 Negatives

It is easy to make sentences negative in Spanish, just put **no** in front of the verb: **No somos americanos** (We're not American).

la bicicleta
lah beethee<u>kle</u>tah
bicycle

I'm not Spanish.	**No soy español.** noh soy espan<u>yol</u>
He's not vegetarian.	**No es vegetariano.** noh es be-hetar<u>ya</u>noh
We don't have any children.	**No tenemos niños.** noh te<u>nay</u>mos <u>neen</u>yos

No tengo coche.
noh <u>ten</u>goh <u>ko</u>chay
I don't have a car.

Repase y repita
Review and repeat

1 How many?

1 tres
tres

2 nueve
<u>nwe</u>bay

3 cuatro
<u>kwa</u>troh

4 dos
dos

5 ocho
<u>o</u>choh

6 diez
dy<u>eth</u>

7 cinco
<u>theen</u>koh

8 siete
<u>sye</u>tay

9 six
seys

1 How many?

Cover the answers with the flap. Then say these Spanish numbers out loud. Check you have remembered the Spanish correctly.

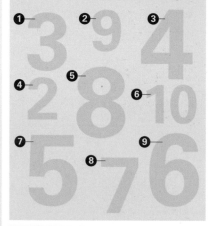

2 Hello

1 **Buenos días. Me llamo... [your name].**
<u>bwe</u>nos <u>dee</u>yas.
may <u>ya</u>moh...

2 **Encantado/-a.**
enkan-<u>ta</u>doh/-ah

3 **Sí, y tengo dos hijos. ¿Y usted?**
see, ee <u>ten</u>goh
dos <u>ee</u>-hos. ee
oos<u>ted</u>

4 **Adiós. Hasta mañana.**
addy-<u>os</u>. <u>as</u>tah
man<u>ya</u>nah

2 Hello

You are talking to someone you have just met. Join in the conversation, replying in Spanish following the English prompts.

Buenos días. Me llamo María.
1 *Answer the greeting and give your name.*

Éste es mi marido, Juan.
2 *Say "Pleased to meet you".*

¿Está usted casado/-a?
3 *Say "Yes, and I have two sons. And you?"*

Nosotros tenemos tres hijos.
4 *Say "Goodbye. See you tomorrow".*

3 To have or be

Fill in the blanks with the correct form of
tener (*to have*) or **ser** (*to be*). Check you have
remembered the Spanish correctly.

1 Yo _____ inglesa.

2 Nosotros _____ cuatro
niños.

3 Yo no _____ feliz.

4 ¿ _____ tú coche?

5 Él _____ mi marido.

6 Yo no _____ teléfono
móvil.

7 Tú no _____
español.

8 ¿ _____ usted
hijos?

3 To have or be

1 **soy**
soy

2 **tenemos**
tenaymos

3 **soy**
soy

4 **tienes**
tyenes

5 **es**
es

6 **tengo**
tengoh

7 **eres**
eh-res

8 **tiene**
tyenay

4 Family

Say the Spanish for each of the numbered
family members. Check you have
remembered the Spanish correctly.

① sister
② grandfather
③ father
④ brother
⑤ grandmother
⑥ daughter
⑦ mother
⑧ son

4 Family

1 **la hermana**
lah airmanah

2 **el abuelo**
el abweloh

3 **el padre**
el pahdray

4 **el hermano**
el airmanoh

5 **la abuela**
lah abwelah

6 **la hija**
lah ee-hah

7 **la madre**
lah mahdray

8 **el hijo**
el ee-hoh

1 Warm up

Count to ten.
(pp.10–11)

Remind yourself how to say "hello" and "goodbye". (pp.8–9)

Ask "Do you have a son?" (pp.14–15)

En la cafetería
In the café

In a Spanish café you can get bread and pastries with your coffee in the mornings. **Churros** (fried dough sticks) are a typical Spanish snack. You can either sit at the counter or have waiter service at a table. It is usual to tip the waiter, but a few coins is usually enough.

2 Words to remember

Familiarize yourself with these words.

el chocolate
el choko<u>la</u>tay
chocolate

el té con limón el tay kon lee<u>mon</u>	*tea with lemon*
el café descafeinado el ka<u>fay</u> deskafey<u>na</u>doh	*decaffeinated coffee*
el cortado el kor<u>ta</u>doh	*espresso with a bit of milk*
la mermelada lah merme<u>la</u>dah	*jam*
la tostada con mantequilla lah tos<u>ta</u>dah kon mante<u>kee</u>-yah	*toast with butter*

el café solo
el ka<u>fay</u> <u>so</u>loh
espresso

Cultural tip A standard coffee is small and black; if you want it any other way, you'll need to specify. If you want tea with milk, ask for "té con leche". If you just ask for "té", you are likely to get tea with lemon.

3 In conversation

Buenos días. Me pone un café con leche.
<u>bwe</u>nos <u>dee</u>yas. may <u>po</u>nay oon ka<u>fay</u> kon <u>le</u>chay

Hello. I'll have a white coffee, please.

¿Eso es todo?
<u>e</u>soh es <u>to</u>doh

Is that all?

¿Tiene churros?
<u>tye</u>nay <u>choo</u>rros

Do you have any churros?

4 Useful phrases ▶

Learn these phrases. Read the English under the pictures and say the phrase in Spanish as shown on the right. Then cover the Spanish with the flap and test yourself.

los churros
los <u>choo</u>rros
churros

el azúcar
el ah-
<u>thoo</u>kar
sugar

el café con leche
el ka<u>fay</u> kon <u>le</u>chay
white coffee

Me pone un café.
may <u>po</u>nay oon ka<u>fay</u>

I'll have a black coffee.

¿Eso es todo?
<u>e</u>soh es <u>to</u>doh

Is that all?

Yo voy a tomar churros.
yoh boy ah to<u>mar</u> <u>choo</u>rros

I'm going to have some churros.

¿Cuánto es?
<u>kwan</u>toh es

How much is that?

Sí, señor.
see, sen<u>yor</u>

Yes, sir.

Gracias. ¿Cuánto es?
<u>grath</u>yas. <u>kwan</u>toh es

Thank you. How much is that?

Cuatro euros, por favor.
<u>kwa</u>troh eh-<u>oo</u>ros, por fa<u>bor</u>

Four euros, please.

Ask "How much is that?" (pp.18–19)

Say "I don't have a brother". (pp.14–15)

Ask "Do you have any churros?" (pp.18–19)

En el restaurante
In the restaurant

There are a variety of different types of eating places in Spain. In a **bar** or **tasca** you can find a few **tapas** or snacks. Lunch is the main meal of the day, but if you are not very hungry, many restaurants offer tapas at the bar, which is usually very good value for a light meal.

2 Words to remember

Memorize these words. Conceal the Spanish with the cover flap and test yourself.

la carta lah <u>kar</u>tah	*menu*
la carta de vinos lah <u>kar</u>tah day <u>bee</u>nos	*wine list*
los entrantes los en<u>tran</u>tes	*starters*
el plato principal el <u>pla</u>toh preen<u>thee</u>pal	*main course*
los postres los <u>pos</u>tres	*desserts*
el desayuno el desah-<u>yoo</u>noh	*breakfast*
el almuerzo el almoo<u>air</u>thoh	*lunch*
la cena lah <u>the</u>nah	*dinner*

cup **7**

knife **6**

5 *spoon*   **4** *fork*

3 In conversation

Hola. Una mesa para cuatro, por favor.
<u>o</u>-lah. <u>oo</u>nah <u>me</u>sah <u>par</u>ah <u>kwa</u>troh, por fa<u>bor</u>

Hello. A table for four, please.

¿Tiene una reserva?
<u>tye</u>nay <u>oo</u>nah re<u>ser</u>bah

Do you have a reservation?

Sí, a nombre de Cortés.
see, ah <u>nom</u>bray day kor<u>tes</u>

Yes, in the name of Cortés.

4 Match and repeat

Look at the numbered objects on this table and match them with the items in the vocabulary list at the side. Read the Spanish words aloud. Now, conceal the list with the cover flap and test yourself.

glass ❶

❽ *saucer*

napkin ❷

plate ❸

1 **la copa**
lah kopah

2 **la servilleta**
lah serbee-yetah

3 **el plato**
el platoh

4 **el tenedor**
el tenedor

5 **la cuchara**
lah koocharah

6 **el cuchillo**
el koochee-yoh

7 **la taza**
lah tathah

8 **el platillo**
el plateeyoh

5 Useful phrases

Learn these phrases and then test yourself using the cover flap to conceal the Spanish.

What do you have for dessert?	**¿Qué tiene de postre?** kay tyenay day postray
The bill, please.	**La cuenta, por favor.** lah kwentah, por tabor

¿Fumadores o no fumadores?
foomadores oh noh foomadores

Smoking or non-smoking?

No fumadores, por favor.
noh foomadores, por fabor

Non-smoking, please.

Síganme, por favor.
seegan-may, por fabor.

Follow me, please.

1 **Warm up**

What are "breakfast", "lunch", and "dinner" in Spanish? (pp.20–1)

Say "I", "you" (informal), "he", "she", "we", "you" (plural/formal), "they" (masculine), "they" (feminine). (pp.14–15)

Querer
To want

Querer (*to want*) is a verb that is essential to everyday conversation. There is also a polite form, **quisiera** (*I'd like*). Use this when requesting something because **quiero** (*I want*) may sound too strong: **¿Qué quiere beber?** (*What do you want to drink?*); **Quisiera una cerveza** (*I'd like a beer*).

2 **Querer: to want**

Say the different forms of **querer** (*to want*) aloud. Use the cover flap to test yourself and, when you are confident, practise the sample sentences below.

yo quiero yoh <u>kya</u>iroh	*I want*
tú quieres/usted quiere too <u>kya</u>ires/oos<u>ted</u> <u>kya</u>iray	*you want (singular, informal/ formal)*
él/ella quiere el/<u>eh</u>-yah <u>kya</u>iray	*he/she wants*
nosotros/-as queremos no<u>sot</u>ros/-as ke<u>ray</u>mos	*we want (masculine/ feminine)*
vosotros/-as queréis/ ustedes quieren bo<u>sot</u>ros/-as ke<u>ray</u>s/ oos<u>ted</u>es <u>kya</u>iren	*you want (plural, informal/ formal)*
ellos/-as quieren <u>eh</u>-yos/-as-yas <u>kya</u>iren	*they want (masculine/ feminine)*

¿Quieres vino? <u>kya</u>ires <u>bee</u>noh?	*Do you want some wine?*
Quiere un coche nuevo. <u>kya</u>iray oon <u>ko</u>chay <u>nwe</u>boh	*She wants a new car.*

Quiero caramelos.
<u>kya</u>iroh kara<u>me</u>los
I want some sweets.

Conversational tip Although it may sound rude to you, Spaniards don't say "please" (por favor) or "thank you" (gracias) very often, and they hardly ever say "excuse me" (perdón) or "I'm sorry" (lo siento), but they use the tone of their voices and choice of words to imply politeness, such as "quisiera" (I'd like) instead of "quiero" (I want).

3 Polite requests

Practise the following sample phrases that use **quisiera** (*I'd like*), the form of **quiero** (*I want*) that is used for polite requests.

I'd like a beer.

Quisiera un cerveza.
kee<u>sy</u>airah oon
ther<u>bay</u>thah

I'd like a table for tonight.

Quisiera una mesa para esta noche.
kee<u>sy</u>airah <u>oo</u>nah <u>me</u>sah parah <u>es</u>tah <u>no</u>cheh

I'd like to see the menu, please

Quisiera ver la carta, por favor.
kee<u>sy</u>airah <u>ber</u> lah <u>kar</u>tah, por fa<u>bor</u>

4 Put into practice

Join in this conversation. Read the Spanish beside the pictures on the left and follow the instructions to make your reply. Then test yourself by concealing the answers using the cover flap.

Buenas tardes señor. ¿Tiene una reserva?
<u>bwe</u>nas <u>tar</u>des sen<u>yor</u>. <u>tye</u>neh <u>oo</u>nah re<u>ser</u>bah
Good evening, sir. Do you have a reservation?

Say: No, but I would like a table for three.

No, pero quisiera una mesa para tres.
noh, peroh kee<u>sy</u>airah <u>oo</u>nah <u>me</u>sah <u>pa</u>rah tres

Muy bien. ¿Qué mesa le gustaría?
mwee byen. kay <u>me</u>sah le goosta<u>ree</u>yah
Very good. Which table would you like?

Say: Near the window please.

Cerca de la ventana, por favor.
<u>ther</u>kah day lah ben<u>ta</u>nah, por fa<u>bor</u>

Los platos
Dishes

1 Warm up

Say "She's happy" and "I'm not sure". (pp.14–15)

Ask "Do you have churros?" (pp.18–19)

Say "I'd like a white coffee". (pp.18–19)

Spain offers a large variety of regional dishes. Plenty of garlic and olive oil are a feature of many typical dishes. Not many restaurants offer a vegetarian menu, but there are, however, many traditional Spanish dishes that do not contain meat. Ask your waiter for advice.

Cultural tip At lunch time, you will find many restaurants offer "el menú del día" (the day's set menu). This is usually a three-course meal with bread and drink included in the price.

2 Match and repeat

Match the numbered items to the Spanish words in the panel.

1 **las verduras**
   las ber<u>doo</u>ras

2 **la fruta**
   lah <u>froo</u>tah

3 **el queso**
   el <u>ke</u>soh

4 **los frutos secos**
   los <u>froo</u>tos <u>se</u>kos

5 **la sopa**
   lah <u>so</u>pah

6 **las aves**
   las <u>ah</u>bes

7 **el pescado**
   el pes<u>ka</u>doh

8 **la pasta**
   lah <u>pas</u>tah

9 **el marisco**
   el ma<u>rees</u>koh

10 **la carne**
    lah <u>kar</u>nay

❶ *vegetables*
❷ *fruit*
❸ *cheese*
❺ *soup*
❻ *poultry*
❽ *pasta*
❾ *seafood*

3 Words to remember: cooking methods

The ending often varies depending on the gender of item described.

Quisiera mi filete bien hecho.
keesyairah mee feeletay byen <u>eh</u>-choh
I'd like my steak well done.

fried (m/f)	**frito/-a** <u>free</u>toh/-ah
grilled	**a la plancha** ah lah <u>plan</u>chah
roasted (m/f)	**asado/-a** ah<u>sa</u>doh/-ah
boiled (m/f)	**hervido/-a** er<u>bee</u>doh/-ah
steamed	**al vapor** al ba<u>por</u>
rare (m/f)	**poco hecho/-a** pokoh <u>eh</u>-choh/-ah

6 Say it

What is "tortilla"?

I'm allergic to seafood.

I'd like a beer.

4 Words to remember: drinks

Familiarize yourself with these words.

water	**el agua** el <u>ah</u>gwah
fizzy water	**el agua con gas** el <u>ah</u>gwah kon gas
still water	**el agua sin gas** el <u>ah</u>gwah seen gas
wine	**el vino** el <u>bee</u>noh
beer	**la cerveza** lah thair<u>bay</u>thah
fruit juice	**el zumo** el <u>thoo</u>moh

④ *nuts*

5 Useful phrases

Learn these phrases and then test yourself.

I am a vegetarian. *(m/f)*	**Soy vegetariano/-a.** soy be-hetar<u>ee</u>anoh/-ah
I am allergic to nuts. *(m/f)*	**Soy alérgico/-a** **a los frutos secos.** soy ah<u>ler</u>-heekoh/-ah ah los <u>froo</u>tos <u>se</u>kos
What is "conejo"?	**¿Qué es "conejo"?** kay es ko<u>ne</u>-hoh

⑦ *fish*

⑩ *meat*

Repase y repita
Review and repeat

Respuestas
Answers
Cover with flap

1 What food?

1 **los frutos secos**
los <u>froo</u>tos <u>se</u>kos

2 **el marisco**
el ma<u>rees</u>koh

3 **la carne**
lah <u>kar</u>nay

4 **el azúcar**
el ah-<u>thoo</u>kar

5 **la copa**
lah <u>ko</u>pah

1 What food?

Name the numbered items.

1 nuts
2 seafood
3 meat
4 sugar
glass **5**

2 This is my...

1 **Ésta es mi mujer.**
<u>es</u>tah es mee
moo-<u>hair</u>

2 **Aquí están sus hijas.**
ah<u>kee</u> es<u>tan</u> soos
<u>ee</u>-has

3 **Su mesa es de no fumadores.**
soo <u>me</u>sah es day
noh fooma<u>do</u>res

2 This is my...

Say these phrases in Spanish.
Use **mi(-s)**, **tu(-us)** or **su(-s)**.

1 *This is my wife.*

2 *Here are her daughters.*

3 *Their table is non-smoking.*

3 I'd like...

1 **Quisiera un café.**
kee<u>sy</u>airah oon
ka<u>fay</u>

2 **Quisiera churros.**
kee<u>sy</u>airah
<u>choo</u>rros

2 **Quisiera azúcar.**
kee<u>sy</u>airah
ah-<u>thoo</u>kar

4 **Quisiera un café con leche.**
kee<u>sy</u>airah oon
ka<u>fay</u> kon <u>le</u>chay

3 I'd like...

Say "I'd like" the following:

1 black coffee
churros **2**   sugar **3**
white coffee **4**

1 What food?

6 **la pasta**
lah *pastah*

7 **el cuchillo**
el koo*chee*-yoh

8 **el queso**
el *ke*soh

9 **la servilleta**
lah serbee-*ye*tah

10 **la cerveza**
lah thair*bay*thah

4 Restaurant

You arrive at a restaurant. Join in the conversation, replying in Spanish following the English prompts.

Buenas tardes señora, señor.
1 *Ask for a table for six.*

¿Fumadores o no fumadores?
2 *Say: non-smoking.*

Síganme, por favor.
3 *Ask for the menu.*

¿Quiere la carta de vinos?
4 *Say: No. Fizzy water, please.*

Muy bien.
5 *Say you don't have a glass.*

4 Restaurant

1 **Buenas tardes, quisiera una mesa para seis.**
bwenas tardes, keesyairah oonah mesah parah seys

2 **No fumadores.**
noh foomadores

3 **La carta, por favor.**
lah *kartah, por fabor*

4 **No. Agua con gas, por favor.**
noh. *ahgwah kon gas, por fabor*

5 **No tengo copa.**
noh *tengoh kopah*

1 Warm up

Say "he is" and "they are". (pp.14–15)

Say "he is not" and "they are not". (pp.14–15)

What is Spanish for "the children"? (pp.10–11)

Los días y los meses
Days and months

In Spanish, days of the week (**los días de la semana**) and months (**los meses**) do not have capital letters. Notice that you use **en** with months: **en abril** (*in April*), but **el** or **los** with days: **el/los lunes** (*on Monday/Mondays*).

2 Words to remember: days of the week

Familiarize yourself with these words and test yourself using the flap.

lunes loones	*Monday*
martes martes	*Tuesday*
miércoles myairkoles	*Wednesday*
jueves hwebes	*Thursday*
viernes byernes	*Friday*
sábado sabadoh	*Saturday*
domingo domeengoh	*Sunday*
hoy oy	*today*
mañana manyanah	*tomorrow*
ayer ah-yair	*yesterday*

Nos reunimos mañana.
mos reh-ooneemos manyanah
We meet tomorrow.

Tengo una reserva para hoy.
tengoh oonah reserbah parah oy
I have a reservation for today.

3 Useful phrases: days

Learn these phrases and then test yourself using the cover flap.

La reunión no es el martes. lah reh-oonyon noh es el martes	*The meeting isn't on Tuesday.*
Trabajo los domingos. traba-hoh los domeengos	*I work on Sundays.*

4 Words to remember: months

Familiarize yourself with these words and test yourself using the flap.

Nuestro aniversario es en julio.
nwestroh aneebairsaree-oh es en hoolee-oh
Our anniversary is in July.

Navidad es en diciembre.
nabeedad es en deethyembray
Christmas is in December.

January	**enero**	ehneroh
February	**febrero**	febreroh
March	**marzo**	marthoh
April	**abril**	abreel
May	**mayo**	mah-yoh
June	**junio**	hoonee-oh
July	**julio**	hoolee-oh
August	**agosto**	agostoh
September	**septiembre**	septyembray
October	**octubre**	oktoobray
November	**noviembre**	nobyembray
December	**diciembre**	deethyembray
month	**el mes**	el mes
year	**el año**	el anyoh

5 Useful phrases: months

Learn these phrases and then test yourself using the cover flap.

My children are on holiday in August.	**Mis hijos están de vacaciones en agosto.** mees ee-hos estan day bakathyones en agostoh
My birthday is in June.	**Mi cumpleaños es en junio.** mee koomplay-anyos es en hoonee-oh

1 Warm up

Count in Spanish from 1 to 10. (pp.10–11)

Say "I have a reservation". (pp.20–1)

Say "The meeting is on Wednesday". (pp.28–9)

La hora y los números
Time and numbers

The hour is preceded by **la** as in **la una** (*one o'clock*) and **las** for the other numbers: **las dos**, **las tres**, and so on. In English the minutes come first: *ten to five*, in Spanish the hour comes first: **las cinco menos diez** (*"five minus ten"*).

2 Words to remember: time

Memorize how to tell the time in Spanish.

la una lah <u>oo</u>nah	*one o'clock*
la una y cinco lah <u>oo</u>nah ee <u>theen</u>koh	*five past one*
la una y cuarto lah <u>oo</u>nah ee <u>kwar</u>toh	*quarter past one*
la una y media lah <u>oo</u>nah ee <u>me</u>dee-ah	*half past one*
la una y veinte lah <u>oo</u>nah ee <u>beyn</u>tay	*twenty past one*
las dos menos cuarto las dos <u>me</u>nos <u>kwar</u>toh	*quarter to two*
las dos menos diez las dos <u>me</u>nos d<u>yeth</u>	*ten to two*

3 Useful phrases

Learn these phrases and then test yourself using the cover flap.

¿Qué hora es? kay <u>o</u>rah es	*What time is it?*
¿A qué hora quiere el desayuno? ah kay <u>o</u>rah <u>kyai</u>ray el desah-<u>yoo</u>noh	*What time do you want breakfast?*
La reunión es a mediodía. lah reh-oon<u>yon</u> es ah maydyo<u>dee</u>-ah	*The meeting is at midday.*

4 Words to remember: higher numbers

To say 21 you use veinti and add **uno** (*one*): **veintiuno**. Successive numbers are created in the same way – for example, **veintidós** (22), **veintitrés** (23), and so on. After 30 link the numbers with **y** (*and*): **treinta y uno** (31), **cuarenta y cinco** (45), **sesenta y seis** (66).

Note the special forms used for 500, 700, and 900: **quinientos**, **setecientos**, and **novecientos**.

Quiero el autobús cincuenta y tres.
<u>kyai</u>roh el aooto<u>boos</u>
theen<u>kwen</u>tah ee tres
I want the number 33 bus.

eleven	**once** <u>on</u>thay
twelve	**doce** <u>do</u>thay
thirteen	**trece** <u>tre</u>thay
fourteen	**catorce** ka<u>tor</u>thay
fifteen	**quince** <u>keen</u>thay
sixteen	**dieciséis** deeaythee<u>sey</u>ees
seventeen	**diecisiete** deeaythee<u>syey</u>tay
eighteen	**dieciocho** deeayth<u>yo</u>choh
nineteen	**diecinueve** deeaythyn<u>we</u>bay
twenty	**veinte** <u>beyn</u>tay
thirty	**treinta** <u>treyn</u>tah
forty	**cuarenta** kwa<u>ren</u>tah
fifty	**cincuenta** theen<u>kwen</u>tah
sixty	**sesenta** se<u>sen</u>tah
seventy	**setenta** se<u>ten</u>tah
eighty	**ochenta** o<u>chen</u>tah
ninety	**noventa** no<u>ben</u>tah
hundred	**cien** <u>thee</u>ayn
two hundred	**doscientos** dos-<u>theeayn</u>tos
five hundred	**quinientos** keeneeayntos
thousand	**mil** meel
two thousand	**dos mil** dos meel
one million	**un millón** oon mee-<u>yon</u>

5 Say It

25

68

84

91

five to ten.

half past eleven.

What time is lunch?

1 Warm up

Say the days of the week. (pp.28–9)

Say "three o'clock". (pp.30–1)

What's the Spanish for "today", "tomorrow", and "yesterday"? (pp.28–9)

Las citas
Appointments

Business in Spain is generally conducted more formally than in Britain or the United States. The Spanish also tend to leave the office for the lunch hour, often having a sit-down meal. Remember to use the formal forms of "you" (**usted**, **ustedes**) in business situations.

2 Useful phrases

Learn these phrases and then test yourself.

¿Nos reunimos mañana? nos reh-ooneemos manyanah	*Shall we meet tomorrow?*
¿Con quién? kon kee-en	*With whom?*
¿Cuándo está libre? kwandoh esta leebray	*When are you free?*
Lo siento, estoy ocupado(-a). loh syentoh, estoy okoopadoh(-ah)	*I'm sorry, I am busy.*
¿Qué tal el jueves? keh tal el hwebes	*How about Thursday?*
A mí me va bien. ah mee may bah byen	*That's good for me.*

el apretón de manos
el apreton day manos
handshake

Bienvenido.
byenveneedoh
Welcome.

3 In conversation

Buenos días. Tengo una cita.
bwenos deeyas. tengoh oonah theetah

Good morning. I have an appointment.

¿Con quién es la cita?
kon kee-en es lah theetah

With whom is the appointment?

Con el Señor Montoya.
kon el senyor montoyah

With Mr Montoya.

4 Put into practice ▷

Join in this conversation. Read the Spanish beside the pictures on the left and then follow the instructions to make your reply. Then test yourself by concealing the answers on the right with the cover flap.

	¿Nos reunimos el jueves? nos reh-oo<u>nee</u>mos el <u>hwe</u>bes? *Shall we meet Thursday?* Say: Sorry, I'm busy.	**Lo siento, estoy ocupado(-a).** loh <u>syen</u>toh, es<u>toy</u> okoo<u>pa</u>doh(-ah)
	¿Cuándo está libre? <u>kwan</u>doh es<u>ta</u> <u>lee</u>bray *When are you free?* Say: Tuesday afternoon.	**El martes por la tarde.** el <u>mar</u>tes por lah <u>tar</u>day
	A mí me va bien. ah <u>mee</u> may bah byen *That's good for me.* Ask: At what time?	**¿A qué hora?** ah kay <u>o</u>rah
	A las cuatro, si a usted le va bien. ah las <u>kwa</u>troh, see ah oos<u>ted</u> le bah byen *At four o'clock, if that's good for you.* Say: Yes, it's good for me.	**Sí, me va bien.** see, may bah byen

Muy bien. ¿A qué hora?
mwee byen. ah kay <u>o</u>rah?

Very good. What time?

A las tres, pero llego un poco tarde.
ah las tres, <u>pe</u>roh <u>ye</u>goh oon <u>po</u>koh <u>tar</u>day

At three o'clock, but I'm a little late.

No se preocupe. Tome asiento, por favor.
noh say pre-oh<u>koo</u>pay. <u>to</u>may as<u>yain</u>toh, por fa<u>bor</u>

Don't worry. Take a seat, please.

Por teléfono
On the telephone

1 Warm up

Say "I'm sorry".
(pp.32–3)

What is the Spanish
for "I'd like an
appointment".
(pp.32–3)

How do you say
"when?" in Spanish?
(pp.32–3)

The emergency number for police,
ambulance, or fire services is 112.
For directory enquiries dial 11818.
Telephone cards can be used with
public or private phones by tapping
in a code. Available from newsagents
and tobacconists, they are a cheap
way to call overseas.

2 Match and repeat

Match the numbered items to the Spanish
in the panel on the left, then test yourself.

1 **el cargador**
el kar<u>ga</u>dor

charger ❶

2 **el contestador
automático**
el kontes<u>ta</u>dor
aoot<u>o</u>mateekoh

3 **la tarjeta
telefónica**
lah tar<u>he</u>tah
tele<u>fo</u>neekah

4 **el móvil**
el <u>mo</u>beel

5 **los auriculares**
los aooreekoo<u>la</u>res

mobile ❹

headphones ❺   *phone card* ❸

3 In conversation

**Dígame, Susana
Castillo al habla.**
<u>dee</u>gamay, soo<u>sa</u>nah
kas<u>tee</u>yoh al <u>ab</u>lah

*Hello. Susana Castillo
speaking.*

**Buenos días. Quisiera
hablar con Julián
López, por favor.**
<u>bwe</u>nos <u>dee</u>yas.
kee<u>sya</u>ir-ah <u>ab</u>lar kon
hoo<u>lee</u>an <u>lo</u>peth, por
fa<u>bor</u>

*Hello. I'd like to speak
to Julián López, please.*

¿De parte de quién?
day <u>par</u>tay day kee-<u>en</u>?

Who's speaking?

4 Useful phrases

Practise these phrases and then test yourself using the cover flap.

Quisiera una línea externa.
kee<u>syai</u>rah <u>oo</u>nah <u>lee</u>neah ex<u>ter</u>nah

I'd like an outside line.

Quiero llamar a cobro revertido.
<u>kye</u>roh ya<u>mar</u> ah <u>ko</u>broh rreber<u>tee</u>doh
I want to reverse the charges.

Quisiera hablar con María Alfaro.
kee<u>syai</u>rah <u>a</u>blar kon ma<u>ree</u>ah al<u>fa</u>roh

I'd like to speak to María Alfaro.

2 *answering machine*

¿Puedo dejar un mensaje?
<u>pwe</u>doh de<u>har</u> oon men<u>sa</u>hay

Can I leave a message?

5 Say it

I'd like to speak to Mr Girona.

Can I leave a message for Antonio?

Perdone, me he equivocado de número.
per<u>do</u>nay, may ay ekeebo<u>ka</u>doh day <u>noo</u>meroh

Sorry, I have the wrong number.

José Ortega, de Imprentas Lacuesta.
ho<u>say</u> or<u>te</u>gah, day eem<u>pren</u>tas la<u>kwes</u>tah

José Ortega of Lacuesta Printers.

Lo siento. La línea está comunicando.
loh <u>syain</u>toh. lah <u>lee</u>neah es<u>tah</u> komoonee<u>kan</u>doh

I'm sorry. The line is busy.

¿Le puede decir que me llame, por favor?
lay <u>pwe</u>day de<u>theer</u> kay may <u>ya</u>may, por fa<u>bor</u>

Can you ask him to call me, please?

Respuestas
Answers
Cover with flap

Repase y repita
Review and repeat

1 Sums

1 **dieciséis**
deeaythee<u>say</u>ees

2 **treinta y nueve**
<u>treyn</u>tah ee
<u>nwe</u>bay

3 **cincuenta y tres**
theen<u>kwen</u>tah ee
tres

4 **setenta y cuatro**
se<u>ten</u>tah ee
<u>kwa</u>troh

5 **noventa y nueve**
no<u>ben</u>tah ee
<u>nwe</u>bay

1 Sums

Say the answers
to these sums out
loud in Spanish.
Then check you
have remembered
correctly.

1 $10 + 6 = ?$

2 $14 + 25 = ?$

3 $66 - 13 = ?$

4 $40 + 34 = ?$

5 $90 + 9 = ?$

3 Telephones

What are the numbered
items in Spanish?

mobile **1**

phone card **3**

2 I want...

1 **Quiere**
<u>kyai</u>ray

2 **quiere**
<u>kyai</u>ray

3 **queremos**
ke<u>ray</u>mos

4 **quieres**
<u>kyai</u>res

5 **quieren**
<u>kyai</u>ren

6 **quiero**
<u>kyai</u>roh

2 I want...

Fill the gaps with
the correct form of
querer (*to want*).

1 ¿ _____ usted un
café?

2 Ella _____ ir de
vacaciones.

3 Nosotros _____ una mesa para tres.

4 Tú _____ una cerveza.

5 Ellos _____ una mesa para dos.

6 Yo _____ caramelos.

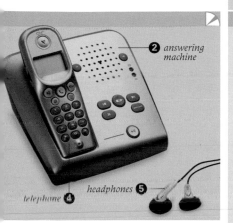

answering machine **2**

telephone **4**   *headphones* **5**

3 Telephones

1 **el móvil**
el mobeel

2 **el contestador automatico**
el kontestador aootomateekoh

3 **la tarjeta telefónica**
lah tarhetah telefoneekah

4 **el teléfono**
el telefonoh

5 **los auriculares**
los aööreekoolares

4 When?

What do these sentences mean?

1 Tengo una cita el lunes veinte de mayo.

2 Mi cumpleaños es en septiembre.

3 Hoy es domingo.

4 No trabajo en agosto.

4 When?

1 *I have a meeting on Monday 20th May.*

2 *My birthday is in September.*

3 *Today is Sunday.*

4 *I don't work in August.*

5 Time

Say these times in Spanish.

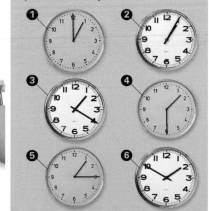

5 Time

1 **la una**
lah oonah

2 **la una y cinco**
la oonah ee theenkoh

3 **la una y veinte**
lah oonah ee beyntay

4 **la una y media**
lah oonah ee medee-ah

5 **la una y cuarto**
lah oonah ee kwartoh

6 **las dos menos diez**
las dos menos dyeth

Count to 100 in tens.
(pp.10–11, pp.30–1)

Ask "What time is it?"
(pp.30–1)

Say "Half-past one".
(pp.30–1)

En la oficina de billetes
At the ticket office

In Spain, commuter trains are very good value, clean, and efficient. Long-distance trains still offer smoking and non-smoking carriages, and the prices vary depending on what day you travel, blue days being the cheapest.

2 Words to remember

Learn these words and then test yourself.

la estación lah estath<u>yon</u>	*(train) station*
la terminal lah termee<u>nal</u>	*(bus) station*
el billete el bee<u>ye</u>tay	*ticket*
de ida day <u>ee</u>dah	*single*
de ida y vuelta day <u>ee</u>dah ee <u>bwel</u>tah	*return*
de primera day preem<u>e</u>rah	*first class*
de segunda day seg<u>oon</u>dah	*second class*
el descuento el des<u>kwen</u>toh	*discount*

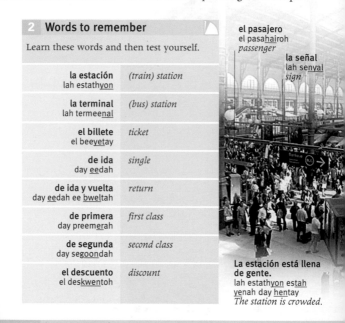

el pasajero
el pasa<u>hai</u>roh
passenger

la señal
lah sen<u>yal</u>
sign

La estación está llena de gente.
lah estath<u>yon</u> est<u>ah</u>
<u>ye</u>nah day <u>hen</u>tay
The station is crowded.

3 In conversation

Dos billetes para Bilbao, por favor.
dos bee<u>ye</u>tes <u>pa</u>rah
beeba-oh, por fa<u>bor</u>

Two tickets for Bilbao, please.

¿De ida y vuelta?
day <u>ee</u>dah y <u>bwel</u>tah

Return?

Si.¿Necesito reservar asiento?
see. neth<u>ese</u>etoh
rreseer<u>bar</u> as<u>yain</u>toh

Yes. Do I need to reserve seats?

4 Useful phrases

Learn these phrases and then test yourself using the cover flap.

	How much is a ticket to Madrid?	**¿Cuánto cuesta un billete para Madrid?** kwantoh kwaystah oon beeyetay parah madreed
	Can I pay by credit card?	**¿Puedo pagar con tarjeta de crédito?** pwedoh pagar kon tarhetah day kredeetoh
Mi tren va con retraso. mee tren bah kon rretrasoh *My train is late.*	Do I have to change?	**¿Tengo que cambiar?** tengoh kay kambee-ar
el tren el andén el tren el anden *train platform*	Which platform does the train leave from?	**¿De qué andén sale el tren?** day kay anden salay el tren
	Are there any discounts?	**¿Hay algún descuento?** ah-ee algoon deskwentoh
	What time does the train for Gijón leave?	**¿A qué hora sale el tren para Gijón?** ah kay orah salay el tren parah geehon

5 Say it

Which platform does the train for Madrid leave from?

Three return tickets to Murcia, please.

Cultural tip

Most train stations now have automatic ticket machines that will often also take credit cards.

No hace falta. Cuarenta euros, por favor. noh ahthay faltah. kwarentah eh-ooros, por fabor

That's not necessary. Forty euros, please.

¿Aceptan tarjetas de crédito? ahtheptan tarhetas day kredeetoh

Do you accept credit cards?

Si. El tren sale del andén cinco. see. el tren salay del anden theenkoh

Yes. The train leaves from platform five.

1 Warm up

What is "train" in Spanish? (pp.38–9)

What does "¿De qué andén sale el tren?" mean? (pp.38–9)

Ask "When are you free?" (pp.32–3)

Ir y coger
To go and to take

The verbs **ir** (*to go*) and **coger** (*to take*) allow you to create many useful sentences. Note that **coger** can also mean to catch: **coger una pelota** (*to catch a ball*), **coger un resfriado** (*to catch a cold*); to grab: **coger a alguien** (*to grab someone*); and to hold: **coger a un bebé** (*to hold a baby*).

2 Ir: to go

Spanish uses the same form of **ir** for both *I go* and *I am going*: **voy a Madrid** (*I am going to Madrid/I go to Madrid*). The same is true of other verbs – for example, **cojo el metro** (*I am taking the metro/I take the metro*).

yo voy yoh boy	*I go*
tú vas/usted va too bas/oosted bah	*you go (informal/ formal singular)*
él/ella va el/eh-yah bah	*he/she goes*
nosotros(-as) vamos nosotros(-as) bamos	*we go*
vosotros(-as) vais/ ustedes van bosotros(-as) baees/ oostedes ban	*you go (informal/ formal plural)*
ellos/ellas van eh-yos/eh-yas ban	*they go*
¿A dónde vas? ah donday bas	*Where are you going?*
Voy a Madrid. boy ah madreed	*I am going to Madrid.*

Voy a la Plaza de España.
boy ah lah plathah day espanyah
I am going to the Plaza de España.

Conversational tip You may have noticed that "de" (of) combines with "el" to produce "del" as in "Museo del Prado" (literally, museum of the Prado); "el menú del día" (menu of the day). In the same way, "a" (to) combines with "el" to produce "al": "Voy al museo" (I'm going to the museum). With feminine and plural words "de" remains separate from "la", "los", and "las".

3 Coger: to take

Say the present tense of **coger** (*to take*) aloud. Use the cover flap to test yourself. When you are confident, practise the sentences below.

yo cojo yoh <u>koh</u>oh	*I take*
tú coges/usted coge too <u>koh</u>es/oos<u>ted</u> <u>koh</u>ay	*you take (informal/ formal singular)*
él/ella coge el/<u>eh</u>-yah <u>koh</u>ay	*he/she takes*
nosotros(-as) cogemos no<u>sot</u>ros(-as) koh<u>ay</u>mos	*we take*
vosotros(-as) cogéis/ustedes cogen bo<u>sot</u>ros(-as) kohe-<u>ees</u>/ oos<u>ted</u>es <u>koh</u>en	*you take (informal/ formal plural)*
ellos/ellas cogen <u>eh</u>-yos/<u>eh</u>-yas <u>koh</u>en	*they take*

Yo cojo el metro todos los días.
yoh <u>koh</u>oh el <u>met</u>roh <u>tod</u>os los <u>dee</u>yas
I take the metro every day.

No quiero coger un taxi. noh <u>kyai</u>roh <u>koh</u>er oon <u>tak</u>see	*I don't want to take a taxi.*
Coja la primera a la izquierda. <u>koh</u>ah lah pre<u>emer</u>ah ah lah eeth<u>kyai</u>rdah	*Take the first on the left.*

4 Put into practice

Cover the text on the right and complete the dialogue in Spanish.

¿A dónde va? ah <u>don</u>day bah *Where are you going?* Say: I'm going to the Puerta del Sol.	**Voy a la Puerta del Sol.** boy ah lah <u>pwer</u>tah del sol
¿Quiere coger el autobús? <u>kyai</u>ray <u>koh</u>er el aooto<u>boos</u> *Do you want to take the bus?* Say: No, I want to go by metro.	**No, quiero ir en metro.** noh, <u>kyai</u>roh eer en <u>met</u>roh

Say "I don't want to take a taxi".
(pp.40–1)

Ask "Where are you going?" (pp.40–1)

Say "80" and "40".
(pp.30–1)

Taxi, autobús, y metro
Taxi, bus, and metro

The metro and some buses operate a ticket system where you have to validate your tickets in a machine. There's a standard fare per ride, but you can also buy a **metrobús**, a book of 10 tickets for both buses and metro.

2 Words to remember

Familiarize yourself with these words.

el autobús el aootoboos	*bus/coach*
la taquilla lah takeeyah	*ticket office*
la estación de metro lah estathyon day metroh	*metro station*
la parada de autobús lah paradah day aootoboos	*bus stop*
la tarifa lah tareefah	*fare*
el taxi el taksee	*taxi*
la parada de taxis lah paradah day taksees	*taxi rank*

¿Para aquí el 17?
parah ahkee el deeaytheeseeaytay
Does the number 17 bus stop here?

3 In conversation: taxi

A la Plaza de España, por favor.
ah lah plathah day espanyah, por fabor

Plaza de España, please.

Sí, de acuerdo, señor.
see, day akwairdo, senyor

Yes, certainly, sir.

¿Me puede dejar aquí, por favor?
may pweday dehar ahkee, por fabor

Can you drop me here, please?

4 Useful phrases

Practise these phrases and then test yourself using the cover flap.

I'd like a taxi to go to the Prado.	**Quisiera un taxi para ir al Prado.** keesyairah oon taksee parah eer al prado
When is the next bus?	**¿Cuándo sale el próximo autobús?** kwandoh salay el prokseemoh aootoboos
How do you get to the museum?	**¿Cómo se va al museo?** komoh say bah al moosayoh
How long is the journey?	**¿Cuánto dura el viaje?** kwantoh doorah el beeahay
Please wait for me.	**Espéreme, por favor.** esperemay, por fabor

Cultural tip Metro lines in Madrid are known by numbers and the names of the first and last stations. Look out for the relevant end station. The Madrid metro runs every day between 6.00am and 2.00am.

◄ Metro ►
Sol
LA MALLOR

6 Say it

Do you go near the train station?

Do you go near the Prado?

When's the next bus to Barcelona?

5 In conversation: bus

¿Pasa cerca del museo?
pasah therkah del moosayoh

Do you go near the museum?

Sí. Son 80 céntimos.
see. son ochentah thenteemos

Yes. That's 80 cents.

Avíseme cuando lleguemos.
abeesemay kwandoh yeghemos

Tell me when we arrive.

1 Warm up

How do you say "I have..."? (pp.14–15)

Say "my father", "my sister", and "my parents". (pp.10–11, pp.12–13)

Say "I'm going to Madrid". (pp.40–1)

En la carretera
On the road

Spanish **autopistas** (*motorways*) are fast but can be quite expensive. You will find signs for **el peaje** (*toll payment stations*). These have multiple lanes. Make sure you enter a green lane that allows payment by cash or credit card. Some lanes are for passholders or lorries only.

2 Match and repeat

Match the numbered items to the list on the left, then test yourself.

1 **el maletero**
   el malay*tairoh*

2 **el parabrisas**
   el para*breesas*

3 **el capó**
   el ka*poh*

4 **la rueda**
   lah *rwedah*

5 **el neumático**
   el ne-ooma*teekoh*

6 **la puerta**
   lah *pwertah*

7 **los faros**
   los *faros*

8 **el parachoques**
   el para*chokes*

Cultural tip Some self-service petrol stations can be unmanned. In this case, you usually have to specify how many litres you want and pay by card *before* filling up.

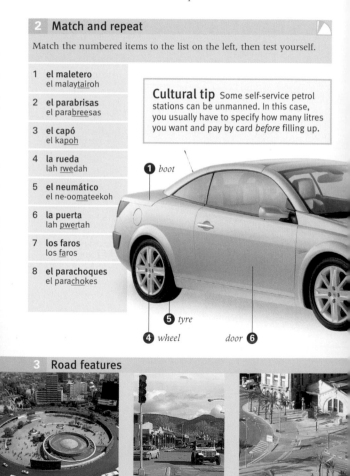

1 boot

5 tyre

4 wheel   door **6**

3 Road features

la rotonda
lah rro*tonduh*

roundabout

el semáforo
el se*maforoh*

traffic lights

el cruce
el *kroothay*

intersection

4 Useful phrases

Learn these phrases and then test yourself using the cover flap.

	The indicator doesn't work.	**El intermitente no funciona.** el intairmeetaintay noh foonthyonah
	Fill it up, please.	**Lleno, por favor.** yennoh, por fabor

5 Words to remember

Familiarize yourself with these words then test yourself using the flap.

6 Say it

There's something wrong with my engine.

I have a flat tyre.

2 windscreen

3 bonnet

7 headlights   bumper 8

petrol	**la gasolina** lah gasoleenah
diesel	**el gasoil** el gasoil
oil	**el aceite** el ah-thayeetay
engine	**el motor** el motor
gearbox	**la caja de cambios** lah kahah day kambyos
indicator	**el intermitente** el intairmeetaintay
flat tyre	**la rueda pinchada** lah rwaydah peenchadah
exhaust	**el tubo de escape** el tooboh day eskapay
driving licence	**el carné de conducir** el karnay day kondootheer

la autopista
lah aootopeestah

motorway/expressway

la autopista de peaje
lah aootopeestah day pyahay

toll motorway

el atasco de tráfico
el ataskoh day trafeekoh

traffic jam

Repase y repita
Review and repeat

1 Transport

1 **el autobús**
el aooto<u>boos</u>

2 **el taxi**
el <u>tak</u>see

3 **el coche**
el <u>ko</u>chay

4 **la bicicleta**
lah beethee<u>klet</u>ah

5 **el metro**
el <u>met</u>roh

1 Transport

Name these forms of transport in Spanish.

bus **①**

metro **⑤**

2 Go and take

1 **ir**
eer

2 **cojo**
<u>ko</u>hoh

3 **va**
bah

4 **vamos**
<u>ba</u>mos

5 **cogen**
<u>ko</u>hen

6 **voy**
boy

2 Go and take

Use the correct form of the verb in brackets.

1 Quiero _____ a la estación. (ir)

2 Yo _____ el metro. (coger)

3 ¿A dónde _____ usted? (ir)

4 Nosotros _____ al Museo del Prado. (ir)

5 Ellos _____ (coger) un taxi.

6 Yo _____ (ir) a Madrid.

2 taxi

3 car

4 bicycle

3 You?

Use the correct form for **usted** or **tú** in each sentence.

1 *You are in a café. Ask "Do you have churros?"*

2 *You are with a friend. Ask "Do you want a beer?"*

3 *A visitor approaches you at your company reception. Ask "Do you have an appointment?"*

4 *You are on the bus. Ask "Do you go near the station?"*

5 *Ask your friend where she's going tomorrow.*

3 You?

1 **¿Tiene churros?**
<u>tye</u>nay <u>choo</u>rros

2 **¿Quieres una cerveza?**
<u>kya</u>ires <u>oo</u>nah thair<u>bay</u>thah

3 **¿Tiene una cita?**
<u>tye</u>nay <u>oo</u>nah <u>thee</u>tah

4 **¿Pasa cerca de la estación?**
<u>pa</u>sah <u>ther</u>kah day lah estath<u>yon</u>

5 **¿A dónde vas mañana?**
ah <u>don</u>day bas man<u>ya</u>nah

4 Tickets

You're buying tickets at a train station. Follow the conversation, replying in Spanish following the numbered English prompts.

¿Qué desea?
1 *I'd like two tickets to Sevilla.*

¿De ida o de ida y vuelta?
2 *Return, please.*

Muy bien. Cincuenta euros, por favor.
3 *What time does the train leave?*

A las tres y diez.
4 *What platform does the train leave from?*

Andén número siete.
5 *Thank you very much. Goodbye.*

4 Tickets

1 **Quisiera dos billetes para Sevilla.**
kees<u>vair</u>ah dos bee<u>ye</u>tes <u>pa</u>rah se<u>bee</u>yah

2 **De ida y vuelta, por favor.**
day <u>ee</u>dah ee <u>bwel</u>tah, por fa<u>bor</u>

3 **¿A qué hora sale el tren?**
ah kay <u>o</u>rah <u>sa</u>lay el tren

4 **¿De qué andén sale el tren?**
day kay an<u>den</u> <u>sa</u>lay el tren

5 **Muchas gracias. Adiós.**
<u>moo</u>chas <u>grath</u>yas. addy-<u>os</u>

En la ciudad
About town

1 Warm up

Ask "How do you get to the museum?" (pp.42–3)

Say "I want to take the metro" and "I don't want to take a taxi". (pp.40–1)

Note that the Spanish word **museo** (*museum*) also means art gallery when it's a public building in which works of art are exhibited; **galería de arte** usually refers to a shop that sells works of art. Be careful, too, not to confuse **librería** (*bookshop* or *bookshelf*) and **biblioteca** (*library*).

2 Match and repeat

Match the numbered locations to the words in the panel.

1 **el ayuntamiento**
   el ahyoonta-<u>myain</u>toh

2 **el puente**
   el <u>pwen</u>tay

3 **el centro**
   el <u>then</u>troh

4 **la iglesia**
   lah eeg<u>les</u>eeah

5 **la plaza**
   lah <u>pla</u>thah

6 **el aparcamiento**
   el aparka-<u>myain</u>toh

7 **la biblioteca**
   lah bibleeo<u>te</u>kah

8 **el museo**
   el moo<u>say</u>oh

❶ *town hall*

❷ *bridge*

church ❹

city centre ❸

❺ *square*

❼ *library*

3 Words to remember

Familiarize yourself with these words and test yourself using the cover flap.

la gasolinera lah gasolee<u>ne</u>rah	*petrol station*
la oficina de información turística lah ohfee<u>thee</u>nah day eenformath<u>yon</u> too<u>rees</u>teekah	*tourist information*
la piscina municipal lah pis<u>thee</u>nah moonee<u>thee</u>pal	*public swimming pool*

Conversational tip In Spanish there are two ways of saying "am", "is", or "are". You have already learned the verb "ser" (p.14): "soy inglés" (I am English); "es vegetariano" (he is vegetarian). When talking about where something is, you need to use a different verb: "estar". The most important forms of this verb are: "estoy" (I am), "está" (he/she/it is), and "están" (they are): "¿Dónde están lla iglesia?" (Where is the church?); "El café no está lejos." (The café isn't far.)

4 Useful phrases

Practise these phrases and then test yourself using the cover flap.

	Is there an art gallery in town?	**¿Hay algún museo de arte en la ciudad?** ah-ee algoon moosayoh day artay en lah thyoodad
	Is it far from here?	**¿Está lejos de aquí?** estah lehos day ahkee

La catedral está en el centro.
lah katedral estah en el thentroh
The cathedral is in the city centre.

There is a swimming pool near the bridge.	**Hay una piscina cerca del puente.** ah-ee oonah peestheenah therkah del pwentay

5 Put into practice

Join in this conversation. Read the Spanish on the left and follow the instructions to make your reply. Then test yourself.

¿Le puedo ayudar? lay pwedoh ahyoodar *Can I help you?*	**¿Hay alguna biblioteca en la ciudad?** ah-ee algoonah beebleeotekah en lah thyoodad
Ask: Is there a library in town?	
No, pero hay un museo. noh, peroh ah-ee oon moosayoh *No, but there's a museum.*	**¿Cómo se va al museo?** komoh say bah al moosayoh
Ask: How do I get to the museum.	
Está por allí. estah por ahyee *It's over there.*	**Muchas gracias.** moochas grathyas
Say: Thank you very much.	

6 *car park*

8 *museum*

1 Warm up

How do you say "near the station"? (pp.42–3)

Say "Take the first on the left". (pp.40–1)

Ask "Where are you going?" (pp.40–1)

Las direcciones
Directions

You'll often be able to find a **mapo de la ciudad** (*town map*) in the town centre, usually near the town hall or tourist office. In the older parts of Latin American towns there are often narrow streets, in which you will usually find a one-way system in operation. Parking is usually restricted.

el bloque de oficinas
el blokay day ohfeeseenas
office block

2 Useful phrases

Learn these phrases and then test yourself.

Dé vuelta a la izquierda/derecha. day vweltah ah lah eeskyairdah/ derechah	*Turn left/right.*
todo recto todoh rrektoh	*straight on*
¿Cómo se va a la piscina? komoh say bah ah lah peesseenah	*How do I get to the swimming pool?*
la primera a la derecha lah preemerah ah lah derechah	*first right*
la segunda a la izquierda lah segoondah ah lah eeskyairdah	*second left*

la fuente
lah fwentay
fountain

3 In conversation

¿Hay un restaurante aquí cerca?
ah-ee oon restaoorantay ahkee serkah

Is there a restaurant nearby?

Sí, cerca de la estación.
see, serkah day lah estasyon

Yes, near the station.

¿Cómo se va a la estación?
komoh say bah ah lah estasyon

How do I get to the station?

4 Words to remember

Familiarize yourself with these words and test yourself using the flap.

Me he perdido.
may eh per<u>dee</u>doh
I'm lost.

el centro deportivo
el <u>sen</u>troh depor<u>tee</u>boh
leisure centre

**la zona
peatonal**
lah <u>son</u>ah
pe-ah<u>ton</u>al
pedestrian zone

traffic lights	**el semáforo** el se<u>ma</u>foroh
corner	**la esquina** lah es<u>kee</u>nah
street/road	**la calle** lah <u>kay</u>ay
main road	**la calle principal** lah <u>kay</u>ay preen<u>see</u>pal
at the end of the street	**al final de la calle** al fee<u>nal</u> day lah <u>kay</u>ay
map	**el mapa** el <u>ma</u>pah
flyover	**el paso elevado** el pasoh ele<u>ba</u>doh
opposite	**enfrente de** en<u>fren</u>tay day

¿Dondé estamos?
<u>don</u>day es<u>ta</u>mos
Where are we?

6 Say it

Turn right at the end
of the street.

Turn left opposite the
museum.

It's ten minutes by
bus.

**Dé vuelta a la izquierda
en el semáforo.**
day <u>vwel</u>tah ah lah
ees<u>kyair</u>dah en el
se<u>ma</u>foroh

*Turn left at the traffic
lights.*

¿Está lejos?
es<u>tah</u> <u>le</u>hos

Is it far?

**No, cinco minutos
andando.**
noh, <u>seen</u>koh
mee<u>noo</u>tos an<u>dan</u>doh

*No, it's five minutes
on foot.*

El turismo
Sightseeing

1 Warm up

Say the days of the week in Spanish. (pp.28–9)

How do you say "six o'clock"? (pp.30–1)

Ask "What time is it?" (pp.30–1)

Many national museums and art galleries close on Mondays. Although shops are normally closed on Sundays, many will open in tourist areas. In provincial areas, it is not unusual for public buildings and shops to close at lunchtime, between 2.00 and 4.00pm.

2 Words to remember

Familiarize yourself with these words and test yourself using the flap.

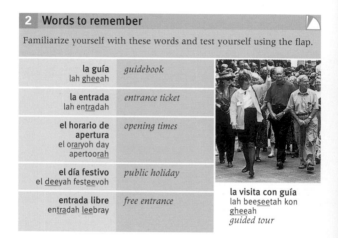

la guía lah gheeah	*guidebook*
la entrada lah entradah	*entrance ticket*
el horario de apertura el oraryoh day apertoorah	*opening times*
el día festivo el deeyah festeevoh	*public holiday*
entrada libre entradah leebray	*free entrance*

la visita con guía lah beeseetah kon gheeah
guided tour

Cultural tip If a public holiday falls on a Thursday or a Tuesday, people will often "hacer puente" (do a bridge). In other words, take Friday or Monday off as well to make a long weekend.

3 In conversation

¿Abren esta tarde? ahbren estah tarday

Do you open this afternoon?

Sí, pero cerramos a las cuatro. see, peroh serramos ah las kwatroh

Yes, but we close at four o'clock.

¿Tienen acceso para sillas de ruedas? tyenen aksesoh parah seeyas day rwedas

Do you have access for wheelchairs?

4 Useful phrases

Practise these phrases and then test yourself using the cover flap.

ABIERTO OPEN	*What time do you open/close?*	**¿A qué hora abre/cierra?** ah kay orah ahbray/syairrah
	Where are the toilets?	**¿Dónde están los baños?** donday estan los banyos
	Is there access for wheelchairs?	**¿Hay acceso para sillas de ruedas?** ah-ee aksesoh parah seeyas day rwedas

5 Put into practice

Cover the text on the right and complete the dialogue in Spanish.

	Lo siento, el museo está cerrado. loh syentoh, el moosayoh estah serradoh *Sorry. The museum is closed.* Ask: Do you open on Tuesdays?	**¿Abren los martes?** ahbren los martes
	Sí, pero cerramos temprano. see, peroh serramos tempranoh *Yes, but we close early.* Ask: At what time?	**¿A qué hora?** ah kay orah

Sí, el elevador está allí.
see, el elaybador estah ah-yee

Yes, there's a lift over there.

Gracias, quisiera cuatro entradas.
grasyas, keesyairah kwatroh entradas

Thank you, I'd like four entrance tickets.

Aquí tiene, y la guía es gratis.
ahkee tyenay, ee lah gheeah es gratees

Here you are, and the guidebook is free.

Say "half past one".
(pp.30–1)

What's the Spanish for
"ticket"? (pp.38–9)

Say "I am going to
New York". (pp.40–1)

En el aeropuerto
At the airport

Although the airport environment is
largely international, it is sometimes
useful to be able to ask your way
around the terminal in Spanish. It's a
good idea to make sure you have a
few coins when you arrive at the
airport; you may need to pay for a
luggage trolley.

2 Words to remember

Familiarize yourself with these words and test yourself using the flap.

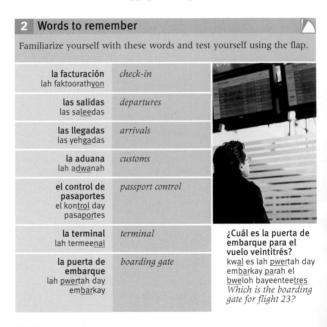

la facturación lah faktoorath<u>yon</u>	*check-in*
las salidas las sal<u>ee</u>das	*departures*
las llegadas las yehg<u>a</u>das	*arrivals*
la aduana lah adw<u>a</u>nah	*customs*
el control de pasaportes el kon<u>trol</u> day pasap<u>or</u>tes	*passport control*
la terminal lah termee<u>nal</u>	*terminal*
la puerta de embarque lah <u>pwer</u>tah day em<u>bar</u>kay	*boarding gate*

**¿Cuál es la puerta de
embarque para el
vuelo veintitrés?**
kwal es lah <u>pwer</u>tah day
em<u>bar</u>kay <u>par</u>ah el
<u>bwe</u>loh bayeentee<u>tres</u>
*Which is the boarding
gate for flight 23?*

3 Useful phrases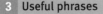

Learn these phrases and then test yourself using the cover flap.

**¿Sale a su hora el
vuelo para Sevilla?**
<u>sa</u>lay ah soo <u>o</u>rah
el <u>bwe</u>loh <u>par</u>ah
se<u>vee</u>yah

*Is the flight for Seville
on time?*

**No encuentro mi
equipaje.**
noh enk<u>wen</u>troh mee
ehkee<u>pa</u>hay

*I can't find my
luggage.*

4 Put into practice

Join in this conversation. Read the Spanish on the left and follow the instructions to make your reply. Then test yourself by concealing the answers using the cover flap.

Hola, ¿le puedo ayudar?
<u>o</u>-lah, lay <u>pw</u>edoh ahyoo<u>dar</u>
Hello, can I help you?

Ask: *Is the flight to Madrid on time?*

¿Sale a su hora el vuelo para Madrid?
<u>sa</u>lay ah soo <u>o</u>rah el <u>bw</u>eloh <u>parah madreed</u>

Sí señor.
see sen<u>yor</u>
Yes sir.

Ask: *Which is the boarding gate?*

¿Cuál es la puerta de embarque?
kwal es lah <u>pw</u>ertah day em<u>bar</u>kay

5 Match and repeat

Match the numbered items to the Spanish words in the panel.

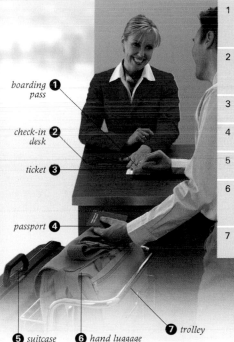

boarding pass **1**

check-in desk **2**

ticket **3**

passport **4**

5 suitcase **6** hand luggage **7** trolley

1 **la tarjeta de embarque**
lah tar<u>he</u>tah day em<u>bar</u>kay

2 **el mostrador de facturación**
el mostra<u>dor</u> day faktoorath<u>yon</u>

3 **el billete**
el bee<u>yeh</u>tay

4 **el pasaporte**
el pasa<u>por</u>tay

5 **la maleta**
lah ma<u>lay</u>tah

6 **el equipaje de mano**
el ehkee<u>pa</u>hay day <u>ma</u>noh

7 **el carrito**
el kar<u>ree</u>toh

Repase y repita
Review and repeat

1 Places

1 **el museo**
el moo<u>say</u>oh

2 **el ayuntamiento**
el ahyoonta-<u>myain</u>toh

3 **el puente**
el <u>pwen</u>tay

4 **la biblioteca**
lah beeblee-oh<u>te</u>kah

5 **el aparcamiento**
el ahparka-<u>myain</u>toh

6 **la catedral**
lah kate<u>dral</u>

7 **la plaza**
lah <u>pla</u>thah

1 Places

Name the numbered places in Spanish.

❶ *museum* ❷ *town hall* ❸ *bridge*

❹ *library* ❺ *car park* ❻ *cathedral*

❼ *square*

2 Car parts

1 **el parabrisas**
el para<u>bree</u>sas

2 **el intermitente**
el intairmee-<u>tain</u>tay

3 **el capó**
el ka<u>poh</u>

4 **el neumático**
el ne-oo<u>ma</u>teekoh

5 **la puerta**
lah <u>pwer</u>tah

6 **el parachoques**
el para<u>cho</u>kes

2 Car parts

Name these car parts in Spanish.

windscreen ❶

❹ *tyre*

❺ *door*

3 Questions

Ask the questions that match these answers.

1 **El autobús sale a las ocho.**
el aooto<u>boos</u> <u>salay</u> ah las <u>ochoh</u>

2 **El café es un euro cincuenta.**
el ka<u>fay</u> es oon eh-<u>ooro</u> theen<u>kwentah</u>

3 **No, no quiero vino.**
noh, noh <u>kyairoh</u> be<u>enoh</u>

4 **El tren sale del andén cinco.**
el tren <u>salay</u> del an<u>den</u> <u>theenkoh</u>

5 **Nosotros vamos a León.**
no<u>sotros</u> <u>bamos</u> ah leh-<u>on</u>

6 **El próximo tren es dentro de quince minutos.**
el <u>prokseemoh</u> tren es <u>dentroh</u> day <u>keenthay</u> <u>meenootos</u>

3 Questions

1 **¿A qué hora sale el autobús?**
ah kay <u>orah</u> <u>salay</u> el aooto<u>boos</u>

2 **¿Cuánto es el café?**
<u>kwantoh</u> es el ka<u>fay</u>

3 **¿Quieres vino?**
<u>kyaires</u> be<u>enoh</u>

4 **¿De qué andén sale el tren?**
day kay an<u>den</u> <u>salay</u> el tren

5 **¿A dónde vais?**
ah <u>donday</u> <u>baees</u>

6 **¿Cuándo es el próximo tren?**
<u>kwandoh</u> es el <u>prokseemoh</u> tren

4 Verbs

❷ *indicator*

❸ *bonnet*

❻ *bumper*

Choose the correct form of the verb in brackets to fill the gaps.

1 **Yo _____ inglés.**
(ser)

2 **Nosotros _____ el metro.** (tomar)

3 **Ella _____ a Marbella.** (ir)

4 **Él _____ casado.** (estar)

5 **¿Tú _____ un té?** (querer)

6 **¿Cuántos niños _____ usted?** (tener)

4 Verbs

1 **soy**
soy

2 **cogemos**
ko<u>haymos</u>

3 **va**
bah

4 **está**
es<u>tah</u>

5 **quieres**
<u>kyaires</u>

6 **tiene**
<u>tyenay</u>

1 Warm up

Ask "Do you accept credit cards?" (pp.38–9)

Ask "How much is that?" (pp.18–19)

Ask "Do you have children?" (pp.10–11)

Reservar una habitación
Booking a room

Types of accommodation in Spain include: **hotel**, categorized from one to five stars; **pensión**, a small family-run hotel; **hostal**, cheap and basic; and **parador**, state-owned hotels in historic properties or places of great beauty.

2 Useful phrases

Practise these phrases and then test yourself by concealing the Spanish on the left using the cover flap.

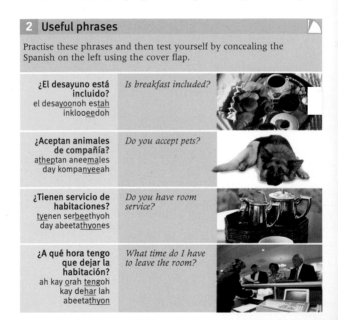

¿El desayuno está incluido? el desa<u>yoo</u>noh es<u>tah</u> inkloo<u>ee</u>doh	*Is breakfast included?*
¿Aceptan animales de compañía? a<u>thep</u>tan anee<u>mah</u>les day kompan<u>yee</u>ah	*Do you accept pets?*
¿Tienen servicio de habitaciones? <u>tye</u>nen ser<u>bee</u>thyoh day abeeta<u>thyo</u>nes	*Do you have room service?*
¿A qué hora tengo que dejar la habitación? ah kay <u>o</u>rah <u>ten</u>goh kay de<u>har</u> lah abeeta<u>thyon</u>	*What time do I have to leave the room?*

3 In conversation

¿Tiene habitaciones libres?
<u>tye</u>nay abeeta<u>thyo</u>nes <u>lee</u>bres

Do you have any vacancies?

Sí, una habitación doble.
see, <u>oo</u>nah abeeta<u>thyon</u> <u>do</u>blay

Yes, a double room.

¿Tiene una cuna? <u>tye</u>nay <u>oo</u>nah <u>koo</u>nah

Do you have a cot?

4 Words to remember

Familiarize yourself with these words and test yourself by concealing the Spanish on the right using the cover flap.

¿Tiene la habitación vistas al parque?
tyenay lah aheetathyon beestas al parkay
Does the room have a view over the park?

room	**la habitación** lah abeetathyon
single room	**la habitación individual** lah abectathyon indeebeedwal
double room	**la habitación doble** lah abeetathyon doblay
bathroom	**el cuarto de baño** el kwartoh day banyoh
shower	**la ducha** lah doochah
breakfast	**el desayuno** el desayoonoh
key	**la llave** lah yabay
balcony	**el balcón** el balkon
air-conditioning	**el aire acondicionado** el ah-eeray akondeethyonadoh

5 Say it

Do you have a single room, please?

For six nights.

Is breakfast included?

Cultural tip Large hotels and paradors are generally the only types of hotel to offer breakfast, but you will generally be charged extra. If your accommodation doesn't provide breakfast, you'll usually find it easy to discover a bar or a café nearby where you can go for "café con leche" in the mornings.

Sí, claro. ¿Cuántas noches?
see, klaroh. kwantas noches

Yes, of course. How many nights?

Para tres noches.
parah tres noches

For three nights.

Muy bien. Aquí tiene la llave.
mwee byen. ahkee tyenay lah yabay

Very good. Here's the key.

1 Warm up

Say "Is there...?" and "There isn't...". (pp.48–9)

What does "¿Le puedo ayudar?" mean? (pp.54–5)

En el hotel
In the hotel

Although the larger hotels almost always have en suite bathrooms, there are still some **pensiones** and **hostales** where you will have to share bathroom facilities and which usually don't provide towels. It is always advisable to check what is provided when you book.

2 Match and repeat

Match the numbered items in this hotel bedroom with the Spanish text in the panel and test yourself using the cover flap.

1 **la mesilla de noche**
   lah me<u>see</u>yah day <u>no</u>chay

2 **la lámpara**
   lah <u>lam</u>parah

3 **el equipo de música**
   el e<u>kee</u>poh day <u>moo</u>seekah

4 **las cortinas**
   las kor<u>tee</u>nas

5 **el sofá**
   el so<u>fah</u>

6 **la almohada**
   lah almoh-<u>ah</u>dah

7 **el cojín**
   el ko<u>heen</u>

8 **la cama**
   lah <u>ka</u>mah

9 **la colcha**
   lah <u>kol</u>chah

10 **la manta**
   lah <u>man</u>tah

❶ bedside table
❷ lamp
❸ music system
❹ curtains
❺ sofa
❻ pillow
❼ cushion
❽ bed
❾ bedspread
❿ blanket

Cultural tip When you arrive in your double room, you will usually see one long pillow instead of two individual ones on the bed. This is the usual pillow for a double bed ("cama de matrimonio" or marriage bed). If you don't want to share your bed or pillow, you'll have to ask for "una habitación doble con dos camas" (a double room with two beds) to get a twin room.

3 Useful phrases

Practise these phrases and then test yourself using the cover flap.

	The room is too cold/hot.	**Hace demasiado frío/calor en la habitación.** _ah_thay daymas_yah_doh _free_oh/_kalor_ en lah abeeta_thyon_
	There are no towels.	**No hay toallas.** noh ah-ee toh-_ah_yas
	I need some soap.	**Necesito jabón.** nethe_seet_oh ha_bon_
	The shower doesn't work.	**La ducha no funciona.** lah _doo_chah noh foon_thyo_nah
	The lift is broken.	**El ascensor está roto.** el asthen_sor_ es_tah_ _rro_toh

4 Put into practice

Practise these phrases and then complete the dialogue in Spanish.

| **¿Le atienden?**
lay at_yain_den
Can I help you? | **Necesito almohadas.**
nethe_seet_oh almoh-_ah_das |
| *Say: I need some pillows.* | |

| **La camarera se las llevará.**
lah kamar_ai_rah say las ye_bar_ah
The maid will bring some. | **Y la televisión no funciona.**
ee lah telebee_syon_ noh foon_thyo_nah |
| *Say: And the TV doesn't work.* | |

1 Warm up

How do you ask "Can I?" (pp.34–5)

Say "The lift is broken".(pp.60–1)

Say "I need some towels". (pp.60–1)

En el cámping
At the campsite

Camping is very popular in Spain. The country's numerous campsites are well organized and operate on a star system. The local tourist information office will be able to offer a list of campsites in the area together with their rating. It is advisable to book in advance during the summer months.

2 Useful phrases

Learn these phrases and then test yourself by concealing the Spanish with the cover flap.

¿Puedo alquilar una bicicleta? pwedoh alkeelar oonah beetheekletah	Can I rent a bicycle?
¿Es el agua potable? es el ahgwah potablay	Is this drinking water?
¿Se permiten hogueras? say permeeten ohgheras	Are campfires allowed?
Las radios están prohibidas. las rradyos estan proheebeedas	Radios are forbidden.

el doble techo
el doblay taychoh
fly sheet

¿Dónde está el grifo?
donday estah el greefoh
Where is the tap?

la oficina
lah ofeetheenah
office

el contenedor de la basura
el kontenedor day
lah basoorah
litter bin

3 In conversation

Necesito una plaza para tres noches.
netheseetoh oonah plathah parah tres noches

I need a pitch for three nights.

Hay una cerca de la piscina.
ah-ee oonah therkah day lah peestheenah

There's one near the swimming pool.

¿Cuánto cuesta para una roulotte?
kwantoh kwestah parah oonah rroolot

How much is it for a caravan?

4 Words to remember

Learn these words and then test yourself using the cover flap.

5 Say it

I need a pitch for four nights.

Can I rent a tent?

Where's the electrical hook-up?

campsite	**el cámping** el <u>kam</u>peen
tent	**la tienda** lah <u>tyen</u>dah
caravan	**la roulotte** lah rroo<u>lot</u>
camper van	**la autocaravana** la ah-ootokara<u>ba</u>nah
pitch	**la plaza** lah <u>pla</u>thah
campfire	**la hoguera** lah oh<u>ghe</u>rah
drinking water	**el agua potable** el <u>ah</u>gwah po<u>ta</u>blay
rubbish	**la basura** lah ba<u>soo</u>rah
camping gas	**el camping-gas** el <u>kam</u>peen gas
showers	**las duchas** las <u>doo</u>chas
sleeping bag	**el saco de dormir** el <u>sa</u>koh day dor<u>meer</u>
air mattress	**la colchoneta** lah kolcho<u>ne</u>tah
ground sheet	**el suelo aislante** el <u>swe</u>loh ah-ees<u>lan</u>tay

los aseos
los a<u>sa</u>yos
toilets

el punto de luz
el <u>poon</u>toh day looth
electrical hook-up

la cuerda
lah <u>kwer</u>dah
guy rope

la clavija
la kla<u>bee</u>hah
tent peg

Cincuenta euros. Una noche por adelantado.
theen<u>kwen</u>tah eh-<u>oo</u>ros. <u>oo</u>nah <u>no</u>chay por adelan<u>ta</u>doh

Fifty euros. One night in advance.

¿Puedo alquilar una barbacoa?
<u>pwe</u>doh alkee<u>lar</u> <u>oo</u>nah barba<u>koh</u>-ah

Can I rent a barbecue?

Sí, pero tiene que dejar una señal.
see, <u>pe</u>roh <u>tye</u>nay kay de<u>har</u> <u>oo</u>nah se<u>nyal</u>

Yes, but you must pay a deposit.

How do you say "hot" and "cold"? (pp.60–1)

What is the Spanish for "room", "bed", and "pillow"? (pp.60–1)

Descripciones
Descriptions

Adjectives are words used to describe things. In Spanish you generally put the adjective after the thing it describes in the same gender and number: **una bebida fría** (*a cold drink*, feminine singular); **un café frío** (*a cold coffee*, masculine singular); **dos bebidas frías** (*two cold drinks*, feminine plural).

2 Words to remember

Adjectives change depending on whether the thing described is masculine (**el**) or feminine (**la**). Generally, a final "o" changes to "a" in the feminine, but if the adjective ends with "e" (such as **grande**) it doesn't change for the feminine. For the plural, just add an "s".

duro/dura dooroh/doorah	*hard*
blando/blanda blandoh/blandah	*soft*
caliente kalyaintay	*hot*
frío/fría freeoh/freeah	*cold*
grande granday	*big*
pequeño/pequeña pekenyoh/pekenyah	*small*
bonito/bonita boneetoh/boneetah	*beautiful*
feo/fea feh-oh/feh-ah	*ugly*
ruidoso/ruidosa rrweedosoh/rrweedosah	*noisy*
tranquilo/tranquila trankeeloh/trankeelah	*quiet*
bueno/buena bwenoh/bwenah	*good*
malo/mala maloh/malah	*bad*
lento/lenta lentoh/lentah	*slow*
rápido/rápida rrapeedoh/rrapeedah	*fast*

las montañas altas
 las montanyas altas
 high mountains

la tienda pequeña
 lah tyaindah pekenyah
 small shop

el coche viejo
 el koche bee-ayhoh
 old car

la calle tranquila
 lah kayay trankeelah
 quiet road

El pueblo es muy bonito.
 el pwebloh es mwee boneetoh
 The village is very beautiful.

3 Useful phrases

Learn these phrases. Note that you can emphasize a description by using **muy** (*very*), **demasiado** (*too*), or **más** (*more*) before the adjective.

This coffee is cold.	**Este café está frío.** estay kafay estah free-oh
My room is very noisy.	**Mi habitación es muy ruidosa.** mee abeetathyon es mwee rrweedosah
My car is too small.	**Mi coche es demasiado pequeño.** mee koche es demasyahdoh pekenyoh
I need a softer bed	**Necesito una cama más blanda.** netheseetoh oonah kamah mas blandah

4 Put into practice

Join in this conversation. Cover up the text on the right and complete the dialogue in Spanish. Check and repeat if necessary.

Ésta es la habitación. estah es lah abeetathyon *This is the bedroom.* *Say: The view is very beautiful.*	**La vista es muy bonita.** lah beestah es mwee boneetah
El cuarto de baño está por ahí. el kwartoh day banyoh estah por ah-ee *The bathroom is over there.* *Say: It is too small.*	**Es demasiado pequeño.** es demasyahdoh pekenyoh
No tenemos otra. noh tenaymos otrah *We haven't another.* *Say: It doesn't matter. We'll take the room.*	**No importa. Nos quedamos con la habitación.** noh importah. nos kedamos kon lah abeetathyon

Repase y repita
Review and repeat

1 Descriptions

1 Descriptions

Put the word in brackets into Spanish. Use the correct masculine or feminine form.

1 **caliente**
   ka<u>lyain</u>tay

2 **pequeña**
   pe<u>ken</u>yah

3 **frío**
   <u>free</u>-oh

4 **grande**
   <u>gran</u>day

5 **tranquila**
   tran<u>keel</u>ah

1 El agua está demasiado _____ (hot).

2 La cama es muy _____ (small).

3 El café está _____ (cold).

4 Este cuarto de baño es más _____ (big).

5 Quisiera una habitación más _____ (quiet).

2 Campsite

2 Campsite

Name these items you might find in a campsite.

1 **el punto de luz**
   el <u>poon</u>toh day looth

2 **la tienda**
   lah <u>tyain</u>dah

3 **el contenedor de la basura**
   el konte<u>ne</u>dor day lah ba<u>soo</u>rah

4 **la cuerda**
   lah <u>kwer</u>dah

5 **los aseos**
   los a<u>say</u>os

6 **la roulotte**
   lah rroo<u>lot</u>

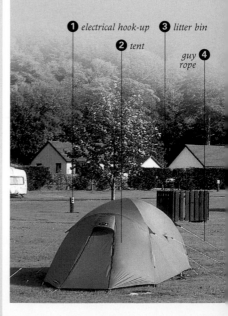

❶ electrical hook-up   ❸ litter bin

❷ tent

guy ❹ rope

3 At the hotel

You are booking a room in a hotel. Follow the conversation, replying in Spanish where you can see the English prompts.

¿Qué desean?
1 *Do you have any vacancies?*

Sí, una habitación doble.
2 *Do you accept pets?*

Sí. ¿Cuántas noches?
3 *Three nights.*

Son ciento cuarenta euros.
4 *Is breakfast included?*

Sí. Aquí tiene la llave.
5 *Thank you very much.*

3 At the hotel

1 **¿Tiene habitaciones libres?**
tyenay abeeta-thyones leebres

2 **¿Aceptan animales de compañía?**
atheptan aneemales day kompanyeeah

3 **Tres noches.**
tres noches

4 **¿El desayuno está incluido?**
el desayoonoh estah inklooeedoh

5 **Muchas gracias.**
moochas grathyas

❺ *toilets*

❻ *caravan*

4 Negatives

Make these sentences negative using the verb in brackets.

1 Yo _____ hijos. (tener)

2 Ellos _____ a Madrid mañana. (ir)

3 Él _____ un café. (querer)

4 Yo _____ el metro. (coger)

5 La vista _____ muy bonita. (ser)

4 Negatives

1 **no tengo**
noh tengoh

2 **no van**
noh ban

3 **no quiere**
noh kyairay

4 **no cojo**
noh kohoh

5 **no es**
no es

1 Warm up

Ask "How do I get to the station?" (pp.50–1)

Say "Turn left at the traffic lights" and "The station is opposite the café". (pp.50–1)

De compras
Shopping

Small, traditional shops are still very common in Spain. But you can also find big supermarkets and shopping centres on the outskirts of cities. Local markets selling fresh, local produce can be found everywhere. Find out the market day from the **oficina de información turística** (*tourist office*).

2 Match and repeat

Match the shops numbered 1 to 9 below and right to the Spanish in the panel. Then test yourself using the cover flap.

1 **la panadería**
   lah panadair<u>ee</u>ah

2 **la pastelería**
   lah pastaylair<u>ee</u>ah

3 **el estanco**
   el est<u>a</u>nkoh

4 **la carnicería**
   lah karnee-thair<u>ee</u>ah

5 **la charcutería**
   lah charkoo-tair<u>ee</u>ah

6 **la librería**
   lah leebrair<u>ee</u>ah

7 **la pescadería**
   lah peskadair<u>ee</u>ah

8 **la joyería**
   lah hoyer<u>ee</u>ah

9 **el banco**
   el b<u>a</u>nkoh

❶ *baker*

❷ *cake shop*

❹ *butcher*

❺ *delicatessen*

❼ *fishmonger*

❽ *jeweller*

Cultural tip If you want an everyday bar of soap or a tube of toothpaste, you need to go to a "droguería" (drugstore) rather than the "farmacia" (pharmacy). The "estanco" (tobacconist) is the place for all sorts of tobacco products and stamps. "Papelerías" cater for all your stationery needs. Most Spanish shops offer a free gift-wrapping service; you only need to ask: "¿Me lo envuelve para regalo?" (May I have it gift-wrapped?).

3 Words to remember

Familiarize yourself with these words and test yourself using the flap.

¿Dónde está la floristería?
donday estah lah floreestaireeah
Where is the florist?

hardware shop	**la ferretería** lah ferretaireeah
antique shop	**el anticuario** el anteekwareeoh
hairdresser	**la peluquería** lah pelookaireeah
greengrocer	**la verdulería** lah berdoolaireeah
post office	**la oficina de correos** lah ofeetheenah day korrayos
shoe shop	**la zapatería** lah thapataireeah
dry cleaner	**la tintorería** lah teentoraireeah
grocer	**el ultramarinos** el ooltramareenos

3 *tobacconist*

6 *bookshop*

9 *bank*

5 Say it

Where is the bank?

Do you sell cheese?

Where do I pay?

4 Useful phrases

Familiarize yourself with these phrases.

Where is the hairdresser?	**¿Dónde está la peluquería?** donday estah lah pelookaireeah
Where do I pay?	**¿Dónde se paga?** donday say pagah
I'm just looking, thank you.	**Sólo estoy mirando, gracias.** soloh estoy meerandoh grathyas
Do you sell phonecards?	**¿Tiene tarjetas telefónicas?** tyenay tarhetas telefoneekas
May I have two of those?	**¿Me pone dos de éstos?** may ponay dos day estos
Can I place an order?	**¿Puedo hacer un pedido?** pwedoh ahther oon pedeedoh

1 Warm up

What is Spanish for 40, 56, 77, 82, and 94? (pp.10–11 and pp.30–1)

Say "I'd like a big room". (pp.64–5)

Ask "Do you have a small car?" (pp.64–5)

En el mercado
At the market

Spain uses the metric system of weights and measures. You need to ask for the produce in kilogrammes or grammes. Some larger items, such as melons or pineapples, tend to be sold by **la pieza** (as single items); other items, such as lettuces, may be sold in lots of two or three.

2 Match and repeat

Match the numbered items in this scene with the text in the panel.

1 **los tomates**
los to<u>ma</u>tes

2 **las judías**
las hoo<u>dee</u>as

3 **los champiñones**
los champee<u>nyo</u>nes

4 **las uvas**
las <u>oo</u>bas

5 **los pepinos**
los pe<u>pee</u>nos

6 **las alcachofas**
las alka<u>cho</u>fas

7 **los guisantes**
los ghee<u>san</u>tes

8 **los pimientos**
los peem<u>yain</u>tos

❶ tomatoes

❺ cucumbers   peas ❼

artichokes ❻   peppers

3 In conversation

Quisiera tomates.
kee<u>sya</u>irah to<u>ma</u>tes

I'd like some tomatoes.

¿De los grandes o de los pequeños?
day los <u>gran</u>des oh day los pe<u>ke</u>nyos

The large ones or the small ones?

Dos kilos de los pequeños, por favor.
dos <u>kee</u>los day los pe<u>ke</u>nyos, por fa<u>bor</u>

Two kilos of the small ones, please.

Cultural tip Spain uses the common European currency, the euro, which is divided into 100 "centimos". Spanish-speaking countries in Central and South America all have their own currencies. Argentina, Chile, Uruguay, Colombia, and México all call their currency the peso, which is divided into 100 "centavos".

❷ *beans*

❸ *mushrooms*

❹ *grapes*

4 Useful phrases

Learn these phrases. Then cover up the answers on the right. Read the English under the pictures and say the phrase in Spanish as shown on the right.

That sausage is too expensive.

Esa salchicha es demasiado cara.
ehsah salcheechah es demasyahdoh karah

How much is that one?

¿A cuánto está esa?
ah kwantoh estah ehsa

5 Say it

Two kilos of peas, please.

The mushrooms are too expensive.

How much are the grapes?

That'll be all.

Eso es todo.
ehsoh es todoh

¿Algo más, señorita?
algoh mas, senyoreetah

Anything else, miss?

Eso es todo, gracias. ¿Cuánto es?
ehsoh es todoh, grathyas. kwantoh es

That'll be all, thank you. How much?

Tres cincuenta.
tres theenkwentah

Three fifty.

1 Warm up

What are these items
you could buy in a
supermarket?
(pp.24–5)

la carne
el pescado
el queso
el zumo
el vino
el agua

En el supermercado
At the supermarket

Prices in supermarkets are usually
lower than in smaller shops. They offer
all kinds of products, with the larger
out-of-town **hipermercados** extending
to clothes, household goods, garden
furniture, and DIY products.

2 Match and repeat

Look at the numbered product categories and match them to the
Spanish words in the panel on the left.

1 **los productos del hogar**
los pro<u>dook</u>tos del oh<u>gar</u>

2 **la fruta**
lah <u>froo</u>tah

3 **las bebidas**
las be<u>bee</u>das

4 **los platos preparados**
los <u>pla</u>tos prepa<u>ra</u>dos

5 **los productos de belleza**
los pro<u>dook</u>tos day be<u>yeth</u>ah

6 **los productos lácteos**
los pro<u>dook</u>tos <u>lak</u>teh-os

7 **la verdura**
lah ber<u>doo</u>rah

8 **los congelados**
los konhe<u>la</u>dos

household products ❶

fruit ❷

drinks ❸

ready meals ❹

vegetables ❼   frozen foods ❽

Cultural tip It is not usually possible to take
unweighed fruit and vegetable sold by the kilo directly to
the supermarket check-out. There is usually a separate
counter or a self-service weighing machine.

3 Useful phrases

Learn these phrases and then test yourself using the cover flap.

May I have a bag, please?	**¿Me da una bolsa, por favor?** may dah <u>oo</u>nah <u>bol</u>sah, por fa<u>bor</u>
Where are the drinks?	**¿Dónde están las bebidas?** <u>don</u>day es<u>tan</u> las be<u>bee</u>das
Where is the check-out, please?	**¿Dónde está la caja, por favor?** <u>don</u>day es<u>tah</u> lah <u>kah</u>hah, por fabor
Please key in your PIN.	**Por favor, meta su PIN.** por fa<u>bor</u>, <u>me</u>tah soo peen

4 Words to remember

Learn these words and then test yourself using the cover flap.

5 beauty products

6 dairy products

bread	**el pan** el pan
milk	**la leche** lah <u>le</u>chay
butter	**la mantequilla** lah mante<u>kee</u>yah
ham	**el jamón** el ha<u>mon</u>
salt	**la sal** lah sal
pepper	**la pimienta** lah pee<u>myain</u>tah
washing powder	**el jabón de lavadora** el ha<u>hon</u> day laba<u>dor</u>ah
toilet paper	**el papel higiénico** el pa<u>pel</u> eehy<u>ain</u>eekoh
nappies	**los pañales** los pa<u>nya</u>les

5 Say it

Where are the dairy products?

May I have some cheese, please?

Where are the frozen foods?

1 **Warm up**

Say "I'd like…".
(pp.22–3)

Ask "Do you have…?"
(pp.14–15)

Say "38", "42", and
"46". (pp.10–11 and
pp.30–1)

Say "big", "small",
"bigger", and
"smaller". (pp.64–5)

La ropa y los zapatos
Clothes and shoes

Clothes and shoes are measured in metric sizes from 36 upwards. Even allowing for conversion of sizes, Spanish clothes tend to be cut smaller than English ones. Clothes size is **la talla** but shoe size is **el número**.

2 Match and repeat

Match the numbered items of clothing to the Spanish words in the panel on the left. Test yourself using the cover flap.

1 **la camisa**
  lah ka<u>mee</u>sah

2 **la corbata**
  lah kor<u>ba</u>tah

3 **la chaqueta**
  lah cha<u>ke</u>tah

4 **el bolsillo**
  el bol<u>see</u>yoh

5 **la manga**
  lah <u>man</u>gah

6 **el pantalón**
  el panta<u>lon</u>

7 **la falda**
  lah <u>fal</u>dah

8 **las medias**
  las <u>me</u>dyas

9 **los zapatos**
  los tha<u>pa</u>tos

shirt **1**

tie **2**

jacket **3**

pocket **4**

sleeve **5**

trousers **6**

Cultural tip As in most of mainland Europe, Spain uses the continental system of sizes. Women's clothes sizes usually range from 36 (UK 8, US 6) through to 46 (UK 20, US 18), and shoe sizes from 37 (UK 4, US 5½) to 45 (UK 11, US 12). For men's shirts, a size 41 is a 16-inch collar, 43 is a 17-inch collar, and 45 is an 18-inch collar.

3 Useful phrases

Practise these phrases and then test yourself using the cover flap.

	*Do you have a larger size?*	**¿Tiene una talla más grande?** tyenay oonah tayah mas granday
	It's not what I want.	**No es lo que quiero.** noh es loh kay kyairoh
	I'll take the pink one.	**Me quedo con el rosa.** may kedoh kon el rrosah

4 Words to remember

Colours are adjectives (pp.64–5) and in most cases have a masculine and a feminine form. The feminine is usually formed by substituting an "a" for the final "o".

red	**rojo/roja** rrohoh/rrohah
white	**blanco/blanca** blankoh/blankah
blue	**azul** athool
yellow	**amarillo/amarilla** amareeyoh/amareeyah
green	**verde** berday
black	**negro/negra** negroh/negrah

⑦ skirt

⑧ tights

⑨ shoes

5 Say it

What shoe size?

Do you have a black jacket?

Do you have size 38?

Do you have a smaller size?

Repase y repita
Review and repeat

Respuestas
Answers
Cover with flap

1 Market

1 **las alcachofas**
las alka<u>cho</u>fas

2 **los tomates**
los to<u>ma</u>tes

3 **los guisantes**
los ghee<u>san</u>tes

4 **los pimientos**
los pee<u>myain</u>tos

5 **las judías**
las hoo<u>dee</u>as

1 Market

Name the numbered vegetables in Spanish.

1 artichokes
2 tomatoes
4 peppers
peas 3
5 beans

2 Description

1 *The shoes are too expensive.*

2 *My room is very small.*

3 *I need a softer bed.*

2 Description

What do these sentences mean?

1 **Los zapatos son demasiados caros.**

2 **Mi habitación es muy pequeña.**

3 **Necesito una cama más blanda.**

3 Shops

1 **la panadería**
lah panadai<u>ree</u>ah

2 **la joyería**
lah hoyeh<u>ree</u>ah

3 **la librería**
lah leebrai<u>ree</u>ah

4 **la pescadería**
lah peskadai<u>ree</u>ah

5 **la pastelería**
lah pastaylai<u>ree</u>ah

6 **la carnicería**
lah karneethai<u>ree</u>ah

3 Shops

Name the numbered shops in Spanish.
Then check your answers.

1 baker
2 jeweller
3 bookshop
4 fishmonger
5 cake shop
6 butcher

4 Supermarket

What is the Spanish for the numbered product categories?

1 *household products*

2 *beauty products*

3 *drinks*

4 *dairy products*

5 *frozen foods*

4 Supermarket

1 **los productos del hogar**
los pro<u>dook</u>tos del <u>oh</u>gar

2 **los productos de belleza**
los pro<u>dook</u>tos day be<u>ye</u>thah

3 **las bebidas**
las be<u>bee</u>das

4 **los productos lácteos**
los pro<u>dook</u>tos <u>lak</u>teh-os

5 **los congelados**
los konhe<u>la</u>dos

5 Museum

Follow this conversation, replying in Spanish following the English prompts.

Buenos días. ¿Qué desean?
1 *I'd like five tickets.*

Son setenta y cinco euros.
2 *That's very expensive!*

No hacemos descuentos a los niños.
3 *How much is a guide?*

Quince euros.
4 *Good. And five tickets, please.*

Noventa euros, por favor.
5 *Here you are. Where are the toilets?*

A la derecha.
6 *Thank you very much.*

5 Museum

1 **Quisiera cinco entradas.**
kee<u>syai</u>rah <u>theen</u>koh en<u>tra</u>das

2 **¡Es muy caro!**
es mwee <u>ka</u>roh

3 **¿Cuánto cuesta una guía?**
<u>kwan</u>toh <u>kwes</u>tah <u>oo</u>nah <u>ghee</u>ah

4 **Bien. Y cinco entradas, por favor.**
Byen, ee <u>theen</u>koh en<u>tra</u>das, por fa<u>bor</u>

5 **Aquí tiene. ¿Dónde están los servicios?**
ah<u>kee</u> <u>tye</u>nay. <u>don</u>day es<u>tan</u> los ser<u>bee</u>thyos

6 **Muchas gracias.**
<u>moo</u>chas <u>gra</u>thyas

Say "from which platform?" (pp.38–9)

What is the Spanish for the following family members: sister, brother, mother, father, son, and daughter? (pp.10–11)

Las ocupaciones
Jobs

Some occupations have commonly used feminine alternatives – for example, **enfermero** (*male nurse*) and **enfermera** (*female nurse*). Others remain the same. When you describe your occupation, you don't use **un/una** (*a*), saying simply **soy abogado** (*I'm a lawyer*), for example.

2 Words to remember: jobs

Familiarize yourself with these words and test yourself using the cover flap. The feminine alternative is shown.

médico medeekoh	*doctor*
dentista denteestah	*dentist*
enfermero/-a enfermairoh/-ah	*nurse*
profesor/-sora profaysor/-sorah	*teacher*
abogado/-a abogadoh/-ah	*lawyer*
contable kontablay	*accountant*
diseñador/-dora deesenyador/-dorah	*designer*
consultor/-a konsooltor/-ah	*consultant*
secretario/-a sekraytareeoh(-ah)	*secretary*
comerciante komerthyantay	*shopkeeper*
electricista elektreetheestah	*electrician*
fontanero/-a fontanairoh/-ah	*plumber*
cocinero/-a kotheenairoh/-ah	*cook/chef*
albañil albanyeel	*builder*
autónomo/-a aootohnomoh/-ah	*self-employed*

Soy fontanero.
soy fontanairoh
I'm a plumber.

Es estudiante.
es estoodyantay
She is a student.

3 Put into practice

Join in this conversation. Read the Spanish on the left and follow the instructions to make your reply. Then test yourself.

¿Cuál es su profesión? kwal es soo profesyon *What do you do?* Say: I am a consultant.	**Soy consultor.** soy konsooltor	
¿Para qué empresa trabaja? parah kay empresah trabahah *What company do you work for?* Say: I'm self-employed	**Soy autónomo.** soy aootohnomoh	
¡Qué interesante! kay intairaysantay *How interesting!* Say: And what is your profession?	**¿Y cuál es su profesión?** ee kwal es soo profesyon	
Soy dentista. soy denteestah *I'm a dentist.* Say: My sister is a dentist too.	**Mi hermana es dentista también.** mee airrmanah es denteestah tambyen	

4 Words to remember: workplace

Familiarize yourself with these words and test yourself.

La oficina central está en Madrid.
lah ofeetheenah thentral estah en madreed
Head office is in Madrid.

branch	**la sucursal** lah sookoorsal	
department	**el departamento** el departamaintoh	
manager	**el jefe** el hefay	
employee	**el empleado** el emplay-ahdoh	
reception	**la recepción** lah rrethepthyon	
trainee	**el aprendiz** el ahprendeeth	

1 Warm up

Practise different ways of introducing yourself in different situations (pp.8–9). Mention your name, occupation (pp.78–9), and any other information you'd like to volunteer.

La oficina
The office

An office environment or business situation has its own vocabulary in any language, but there are many items that are virtually universal. Be aware that Spanish computer keyboards have a different layout to the standard English QWERTY convention; they also include **ñ**, vowels with accents, **¡**, and **¿**.

2 Words to remember

Familiarize yourself with these words. Read them aloud several times and try to memorize them. Conceal the Spanish with the cover flap and test yourself.

el monitor el mon<u>ee</u>tor	*monitor*
el ratón el rra<u>ton</u>	*mouse*
el correo electrónico el ko<u>rray</u>oh elek<u>tro</u>neekoh	*email*
el internet el eenter<u>net</u>	*internet*
la contraseña lah kontra<u>sen</u>yah	*password*
la mensajería de voz lah mensahe<u>ree</u>ah day both	*voicemail*
el fax el fax	*fax machine*
la fotocopiadora lah fotokopya<u>dor</u>ah	*photocopier*
la agenda lah ah-<u>hen</u>dah	*diary*
la tarjeta de visita lah tar<u>het</u>ah day bee<u>seet</u>ah	*business card*
la reunión lah reh-oony<u>on</u>	*meeting*
la conferencia lah konfair<u>en</u>theeah	*conference*
el orden del día el <u>or</u>den del <u>dee</u>ah	*agenda*

1 *lamp*

screen 4

2 *stapler*

telephone 3

pen 10

notepad 11

drawer 12

3 Useful phrases

Learn these phrases and then test yourself using the cover flap.

	I need to make some photocopies.	**Necesito hacer unas fotocopias.** netheseetoh ahther oonas fotokopyas
	I'd like to arrange an appointment.	**Quisiera organizar una cita.** keesyairah organeethar oonah theetah
	I want to send an email.	**Quiero mandar un correo electrónico.** kyairoh mandar oon korrayoh elektroneekoh

4 Match and repeat

Match the numbered items to the Spanish words on the left.

5 *keyboard*

6 *computer*

printer **9**

7 *desk*

8 *clock*

1 **la lámpara**
   lah lamparah

2 **la grapadora**
   lah grapadohrah

3 **el teléfono**
   el telefonoh

4 **la pantalla**
   lah pantayah

5 **el teclado**
   el tekladoh

6 **el ordenador**
   el ordenador

7 **la mesa de escritorio**
   lah mesah day eskreetoryoh

8 **el reloj**
   el rrelokh

9 **la impresora**
   lah impresorah

10 **el bolígrafo**
   el boleegrafoh

11 **el bloc**
   el blok

12 **el cajón**
   el kahon

13 **la silla giratoria**
   lah seeyah heeratoreeah

5 Say it

I'd like to arrange a conference.

I need to send a fax.

Do you have email?

13 *swivel chair*

Say "library" and
"How interesting!"
(pp.48–9, pp.78–9)

Ask "What is your
profession?" and
answer "I'm an
engineer". (pp.78–9)

El mundo
académico
Academic world

In Spain students are selected for a
first degree (**una licenciatura**) by an
average of secondary school grades
and an exam. After graduation some
students go on to **un máster** (master's
degree) or **un doctorado** (PhD).

2 Useful phrases

Practise these phrases and then test yourself using the cover flap.

¿Cuál es su especialidad? kwal es soo espetheeahlee<u>dad</u>	*What is your field?*	
Hago investigación en bioquímica. <u>ah</u>goh inbesteegathy<u>on</u> en beeohkee<u>mee</u>kah	*I am doing research in biochemistry.*	
Soy licenciado en derecho. soy leethenthee<u>ah</u>doh en <u>de</u>rechoh	*I have a degree in law.*	
Voy a dar una conferencia sobre arquitectura. boy ah dar <u>oo</u>nah konfair<u>ayn</u>theeah <u>so</u>breh arkeetek<u>too</u>rah	*I'm going to give a lecture on architecture.*	

3 In conversation

Hola, soy la profesora Fernández.
<u>o</u>-lah, soy lah profay<u>sor</u>ah fer<u>nan</u>deth

Hello, I'm Professor Fernandez.

¿De qué universidad es usted?
deh keh ooneebersee<u>dad</u> es oos<u>ted</u>

What university are you from?

De la Universidad de Murcia.
deh lah ooneebersee<u>dad</u> deh <u>moor</u>theeah

From the University of Murcia.

4 Words to remember

Familiarize yourself with these words and then test yourself.

conference/lecture	**la conferencia**	lah konfair<u>ain</u>theeah
trade fair	**la feria**	lah <u>fe</u>reeah
seminar	**el seminario**	el semee<u>na</u>ryoh
lecture theatre	**el anfiteatro**	el anfeetay-<u>ah</u>troh
conference room	**la sala de conferencias**	lah <u>sah</u>lah deh konfer<u>ain</u>theeas
exhibition	**la exposición**	lah eksposeethy<u>on</u>
library	**la biblioteca**	lah bibleeo<u>te</u>kah
university lecturer	**el profesor de universidad**	el profay<u>sor</u> deh ooneeberseedad
professor	**el catedrático**	el kated<u>ra</u>teekoh
medicine	**medicina**	medeethee<u>na</u>h
science	**ciencias**	<u>thya</u>intheeas
literature	**literatura**	leetaira<u>too</u>rah
engineering	**ingeniería**	inhainyair<u>ee</u>eah

Tenemos un stand en la feria.
tenemos oon estand en la <u>fe</u>reeah
We have a stand at the trade fair.

5 Say it

I'm doing research in medicine.

I have a degree in literature.

She's the professor.

¿Cuál es su especialidad?
kwal es soo espethyalee<u>dad</u>

What's your field?

Hago investigación en ingeniería.
<u>ah</u>goh inbesteegathy<u>on</u> en inhenyair<u>ee</u>eah

I'm doing research in engineering.

¡Qué interesante! Yo también.
keh intairay<u>san</u>tay.
yoh tambee<u>ayn</u>

How interesting! Me too.

1 Warm up

Ask "Can I ...?"
(pp.34–5)

Say "I want to send an email". (pp.80–1)

Say "I'd like to arrange an appointment."
(pp.80–1)

Los negocios
In business

You will receive a more friendly reception and make a good impression if you make the effort to begin a meeting with a short introduction in Spanish, even if your vocabulary is limited. After that, all parties will probably be happy to continue the proceedings in English.

2 Words to remember

Familiarize yourself with these words and then test yourself by concealing the Spanish with the cover flap.

el cliente
el klyaintay
client

el programa el programah	*schedule*
la entrega lah entraygah	*delivery*
el pago el pahgoh	*payment*
el presupuesto el praysoopwestoh	*budget/estimate*
el precio el praythyoh	*price*
el documento el dokoomentoh	*document*
la factura lah faktoorah	*invoice*
la propuesta lah propwestah	*proposal*
los beneficios los baynayfeethyos	*profits*
las ventas las bentas	*sales*
los números los noomeros	*figures*

el informe
el informay
report

Cultural tip A long lunch with wine is still a regular feature of doing business in Spain. As a visiting client you can expect to be taken out to a restaurant, and as a supplier you should consider entertaining your business customers.

3 Useful phrases

Practise these useful business phrases and then test yourself using the cover flap.

¿Firmamos el contrato?
feer*mam*os el kon*trat*oh
Shall we sign the contract?

el ejecutivo
el eh-hekoo*teeb*oh
executive

Please send me the contract.

Me manda el contrato, por favor.
may *mand*ah el kon*trat*oh, por fa*bor*

Have we agreed a schedule?

¿Hemos acordado un programa?
*ehm*os akor*dad*oh oon pro*gram*ah

When can you make the delivery?

¿Cuándo puede hacer la entrega?
*kwand*oh *pwed*ay ah*thor* lah en*treg*ah

What's the budget?

¿Cuál es el presupuesto?
kwal es el praysoo*pwest*oh

Can you send me the invoice?

¿Me puede mandar la factura?
may *pwed*ay mandar lah fak*toor*ah

el contrato
el kon*trat*oh
contract

4 Say it

Can you send me the estimate?

Have we agreed a price?

What are the profits?

Respuestas
Answers
Cover with flap

Repase y repita
Review and repeat

1 At the office

1 **la grapadora**
lah grapa<u>do</u>rah

2 **la lámpara**
lah <u>lam</u>parah

3 **el ordenador**
el ordena<u>dor</u>

4 **el bolígrafo**
el bo<u>lee</u>grafoh

5 **el reloj**
el rre<u>lokh</u>

6 **el bloc**
el blok

7 **la mesa de escritorio**
lah <u>me</u>sah day eskree<u>tor</u>yoh

1 At the office

Name these items.

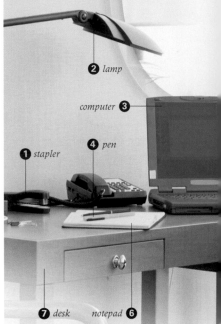

2 lamp

3 computer

4 pen

1 stapler

7 desk   notepad **6**

2 Jobs

1 **médico**
<u>me</u>deekoh

2 **fontanero/-a**
font<u>anai</u>roh/-ah

3 **comerciante**
komerth<u>yan</u>tay

4 **contable**
kon<u>ta</u>blay

5 **estudiante**
estood<u>yan</u>tay

6 **abogado/-a**
abo<u>ga</u>doh/-ah

2 Jobs

What are these jobs in Spanish?

1 *doctor*

2 *plumber*

3 *shopkeeper*

4 *accountant*

5 *student*

6 *lawyer*

clock **5**

3 Work

Answer these questions following the English prompts.

¿Para qué empresa trabaja?
1 Say: I am self-employed.

¿En qué universidad está?
2 Say: I'm at the University of Salamanca.

¿Cuál es su especialidad?
3 Say: I'm doing research in medicine.

¿Hemos acordado un programa?
4 Say: Yes, my secretary has the schedule.

3 Work

1 **Soy autónomo.**
soy aootonomoh

2 **Estoy en la Universidad de Salamanca.**
estoy en lah ooneeberseedad day salamankah

3 **Hago investigación en medicina.**
ahgoh inbesteegathyon en medeetheenah

4 **Sí, mi secretaria tiene el programa.**
see, mee sekretareeah tyenay el programah

4 How much?

Answer the question with the amount shown in brackets.

1 ¿Cuánto cuesta el desayuno? (€3.50)

2 ¿Cuánto cuesta la habitación? (€47)

3 ¿Cuánto cuesta un kilo de tomates? (€3.25)

4 ¿Cuánto cuesta un plaza para cuatro noches? (€60)

4 How much?

1 **Son tres euros cincuenta.**
son tres eh-ooros theenkwentah

2 **Son cuarenta y siete euros.**
son kwarentah ee seeaytay eh-ooros

3 **Son tres euros veinticinco.**
son tres eh-ooros beynteetheenkoh

4 **Son sesenta euros.**
son sesentah eh-ooros

Say "I'm allergic to nuts". (pp.24–5)

Say the verb "tener" (to have) in all its forms: yo, tú, él/ella, nosotros(-as), vosotros(-as), ellos (-as). (pp.14–15)

En la farmacia
At the chemist

Spanish pharmacists are qualified to give advice and sell over-the-counter medicines, as well as dispensing prescription medicines. There is generally a **farmacia de guardia** (duty pharmacy) to provide 24-hour service in every town – a list is displayed in every pharmacy.

2 Match and repeat

Match the numbered items to the Spanish words in the panel on the left and test yourself using the cover flap.

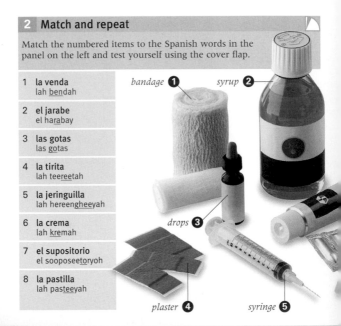

1 **la venda**
lah <u>ben</u>dah

2 **el jarabe**
el ha<u>ra</u>bay

3 **las gotas**
las <u>go</u>tas

4 **la tirita**
lah tee<u>ree</u>tah

5 **la jeringuilla**
lah hereen<u>ghee</u>yah

6 **la crema**
lah <u>kre</u>mah

7 **el supositorio**
el soopo<u>see</u>toryoh

8 **la pastilla**
lah pas<u>tee</u>yah

bandage **1**

syrup **2**

drops **3**

plaster **4**

syringe **5**

3 In conversation

Buenos días, señor. ¿Qué desea?
<u>bwe</u>nos <u>dee</u>yas, sen<u>yor</u>. kay de<u>say</u>ah

Good morning, sir. What would you like?

Tengo dolor de estómago.
<u>ten</u>goh <u>dol</u>or day es<u>to</u>magoh

I have a stomach ache.

¿Tiene diarrea?
<u>tye</u>nay deeah<u>rra</u>yah

Do you have diarrhoea?

4 Words to remember

Familiarize yourself with these words and test yourself using the flap.

headache	**el dolor de cabeza** el do<u>lor</u> day ka<u>be</u>thah
stomach ache	**el dolor de estómago** el do<u>lor</u> day es<u>to</u>magoh
diarrhoea	**la diarrea** lah deeah<u>rra</u>yah
cold	**el resfriado** el rresfree<u>ah</u>doh
cough	**la tos** lah tos
sunstroke	**la insolación** lah eensolatheey<u>on</u>
toothache	**el dolor de muelas** el dolor day <u>mwe</u>las

Tengo dolor de cabeza.
<u>ten</u>goh do<u>lor</u> day
ka<u>be</u>thah
I have a headache.

6 Say it

I have a cold.

Do you have that as a cream?

He has toothache.

6 cream

7 suppository

8 tablet

5 Useful phrases

Practise these phrases and then test yourself using the cover flap.

I have sunstroke.	**Tengo una insolación.** <u>ten</u>goh <u>oo</u>nah eensolatheey<u>on</u>
Do you have that as a syrup?	**¿Lo tiene en jarabe?** loh <u>tye</u>nay en ha<u>ra</u>bay
I'm allergic to penicillin.	**Soy alérgico a la penicilina.** soy aler<u>he</u>ckoh ah lah peneethee<u>lee</u>nah

No, pero tengo dolor de cabeza.
noh, <u>pe</u>roh <u>ten</u>goh do<u>lor</u>
day ka<u>be</u>thah

No, but I have a headache.

Aquí tiene.
ah<u>kee</u> <u>tye</u>nay

Here you are.

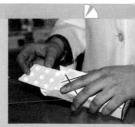

¿Lo tiene en pastilla?
loh <u>tye</u>nay en pas<u>tee</u>yah

Do you have this as pills?

Say " I have toothache" and "I have sunstroke". (pp.88–9)

Say the Spanish for "red", "green", "black", and "yellow". (pp.74–5)

El cuerpo
The body

You are most likely to need to refer to parts of the body in the context of illness – for example, when describing aches and pains to a doctor. The most common phrases for talking about discomfort are **Tengo un dolor en la/el...** (*I have a pain in the...*) and **Me duele la/el...** (*My ... hurts me*).

2 Match and repeat: body

Match the numbered parts of the body with the list on the left. Test yourself by using the cover flap.

1 **la mano**
lah <u>ma</u>noh

2 **la cabeza**
lah ka<u>be</u>thah

3 **el hombro**
el <u>om</u>broh

4 **el codo**
el <u>ko</u>doh

5 **el pelo**
el <u>pe</u>loh

6 **el brazo**
el <u>bra</u>thoh

7 **el cuello**
el <u>kwe</u>yoh

8 **el pecho**
el <u>pe</u>choh

9 **el estómago**
el es<u>to</u>magoh

10 **la pierna**
lah <u>pyair</u>nah

11 **la rodilla**
lah rro<u>dee</u>yah

12 **el pie**
el pee-<u>ay</u>

hand ❶
head ❷
shoulder ❸
❹ elbow
❺ hair
❻ arm
❼ neck
❽ chest
❾ stomach
❿ leg
⓫ knee
⓬ foot

3 Match and repeat: face

Match the numbered facial features with the list on the right.

eyebrow **1**

nose **3**

ear **5**

2 eye

4 mouth

1 **la ceja**
lah <u>thay</u>ah

2 **el ojo**
el <u>oh</u>-hoh

3 **la nariz**
lah na<u>reeth</u>

4 **la boca**
lah <u>bok</u>ah

5 **la oreja**
lah oh<u>ray</u>ah

4 Useful phrases

Learn these phrases and then test yourself using the cover flap.

	I have a pain in my back.	**Tengo un dolor en la espalda.** <u>ten</u>goh oon do<u>lor</u> en lah es<u>pal</u>da
	I have a rash on my arm.	**Tengo un sarpullido en el brazo.** <u>ten</u>goh oon sarpoo<u>yee</u>doh en el <u>brath</u>oh
	I don't feel well.	**No me encuentro bien.** noh may en<u>kwen</u>troh byen

5 Put into practice

Join in this conversation and test yourself using the cover flap.

¿Cuál es el problema?
kwal es el pro<u>blem</u>ah
What's the problem?

Say: *I don't feel well.*

No me encuentro bien.
noh may en<u>kwen</u>troh byen

¿Dónde le duele?
<u>don</u>day lay <u>dwel</u>ay
Where does it hurt?

Say: *I have a pain in the shoulder.*

Tengo un dolor en el hombro.
<u>ten</u>goh oon do<u>lor</u> en el <u>om</u>broh

Say "I need some tablets". (pp.60–1, pp.88–9)

Say "He needs some cream". (pp.88–9)

What is the Spanish for "I don't have a son". (pp.10–15)

En el médico
At the doctor

Unless it's an emergency, you have to book an appointment with the doctor and pay when you leave. You can usually reclaim the money if you have medical insurance. Your hotel, a local pharmacy or tourist information office may be able to tell you the names and addresses of local doctors.

2 Useful phrases you may hear

Practise these phrases and then test yourself using the cover flap to conceal the Spanish on the left.

No es grave. noh es gravay	*It's not serious.*
Necesita hacerse unas pruebas. netheseetah ahthersay oonas prwaybas	*You need to have some tests.*
Tiene una infección de riñón. tyenay oonah infekthyon day rreenyon	*You have a kidney infection.*
Necesita ir al hospital. netheseetah eer al ospeetal	*You need to go to hospital.*

Le voy a dar una receta.
lay boy ah dar oonah rrethetah
I'm going to give you a prescription.

3 In conversation

¿Cuál es el problema?
kwal es el problemah

What's the problem?

Tengo un dolor en el pecho.
tengoh oon dolor en el pechoh

I have a pain in my chest.

Déjeme que la examine.
dayhaymay kay lah eksameenay

Let me examine you.

Cultural tip If you are an EU national, you are entitled to free emergency medical treatment in Spain on production of a European Health Insurance Card or E111 form. For an ambulance, call 112.

4 Useful phrases you may need to say

Practise these phrases and then test yourself using the cover flap.

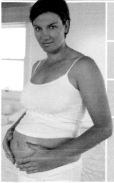

Estoy embarazada.
estoy embarathadah
I am pregnant.

I am diabetic.	**Soy diabético/-a.** soy deeah<u>bet</u>eekoh/-ah
I am epileptic.	**Soy epiléptico/-a.** soy epee<u>lep</u>teekoh/-ah
I'm asthmatic.	**Soy asmático/-a.** soy asmateekoh/-ah
I have a heart condition.	**Tengo un problema de corazón.** <u>ten</u>goh oon <u>pro</u>blemah day kora<u>thon</u>
I have a temperature.	**Tengo fiebre.** <u>ten</u>goh <u>fyay</u>bray
I feel faint.	**Estoy mareado.** estoy maray-<u>ah</u>doh
It's urgent.	**Es urgente.** es oor<u>hen</u>tay

5 Say it

My son is diabetic.

I have a pain in my arm.

It's not urgent.

¿Es grave?
es <u>gra</u>vay

Is it serious?

No, sólo tiene indigestión.
noh, <u>so</u>loh <u>tye</u>nay indeehestyon

No, you only have indigestion.

¡Menos mal!
<u>may</u>nos mal

What a relief!

1 Warm up

Say "How long is the journey?" (pp.42–3)

Ask "Is is serious?" (pp.92–3)

What is the Spanish for "mouth" and "head"? (pp.90–1)

En el hospital
At the hospital

It is useful to know a few basic phrases relating to hospitals and medical treatment for use in an emergency, or in case you need to visit a friend or colleague in hospital. Most Spanish hospitals have only two beds per room and their own en-suite bathroom facilities.

2 Useful phrases

Familiarize yourself with these phrases. Conceal the Spanish with the cover flap and test yourself.

¿Cuáles son las horas de visita? kwales son las oras day beeseetah	*What are the visiting hours?*
¿Cuánto tiempo va a tardar? kwantoh tyempoh bah ah tardar	*How long will it take?*
¿Va a doler? bah ah doler	*Will it hurt?*
Túmbese aquí por favor. toombesay ahkee por fabor	*Please lie down here.*
No puede comer nada. noh pweday komer nadah	*You cannot eat anything.*
No mueva la cabeza. noh mwebah lah kabethah	*Don't move your head.*
Abra la boca por favor. ahbrah lah bokah por fabor	*Please open your mouth.*
Necesita un análisis de sangre. netheseetah oon analeesees day sangray	*You need a blood test.*

el gotero
 el goteroh
 drip

¿Se encuentra mejor?
 say enkwentrah mehor
 Are you feeling better?

¿Dónde está la sala de espera?
 donday estah lah salah day esperah
 Where is the waiting room?

3 Words to remember

Familiarize yourself with these words and test yourself using the flap.

Su radiografía es normal.
soo rradyografeeah es normal
Your x-ray is normal.

emergency department	**el servicio de urgencias** el serbeethyoh day oorhentheeas
x-ray department	**el servicio de radiología** el serbeethyoh day rradyoloheeah
children's ward	**la sala de pediatría** lah salah day pedeeatreeah
operating theatre	**el quirófano** el keerofanoh
waiting room	**la sala de espera** lah salah day esperah
stairs	**las escaleras** las eskaleras

4 Put into practice

Join in this conversation. Cover up the text on the right and complete the anwering part of the dialogue in Spanish. Check your answers and repeat if necessary.

Tiene una infección.
tyenay oonah infekthyon
You have an infection.

Ask: Do I need tests?

¿Necesito hacerme pruebas?
netheseetoh ahthermay prwaybas

Primero necesita un análisis de sangre.
preemeroh netheseetah oon analeesees day sangray
First you will need a blood test.

Ask: Will it hurt?

¿Me va a doler?
may bah ah doler

5 Say it

Does he need a blood test?

Where is the children's ward.

Do I need an x-ray?

No, no se preocupe.
noh, noh say pray-okoopay
No. Don't worry.

Ask: How long will it take?

¿Cuánto tiempo va a tardar?
kwantoh tyempoh bah ah tardar

Respuestas
Answers
Cover with flap

Repase y repita
Review and repeat

1 The body

1 **la cabeza**
lah ka<u>be</u>thah

2 **el brazo**
el <u>bra</u>thoh

3 **el pecho**
el <u>pe</u>choh

4 **el estómago**
el es<u>to</u>magoh

5 **la pierna**
lah <u>pyair</u>nah

6 **la rodilla**
lah rro<u>dee</u>yah

7 **el pie**
el pee-<u>ay</u>

1 The body

Name the numbered body parts in Spanish.

1 head
2 arm
chest 3
4 stomach
leg 5
knee 6
foot 7

2 On the phone

1 **Quisiera hablar con Ana Flores.**
kee<u>syai</u>rah ha<u>blar</u> kon <u>a</u>nna <u>flo</u>res

2 **Luis Cortés de Don Frío.**
<u>looe</u>es <u>kor</u>tes day don <u>free</u>-oh

3 **¿Puedo dejar un mensaje?**
<u>pwe</u>doh de<u>har</u> oon men<u>sa</u>hay

4 **La cita el lunes a las once está bien.**
lah <u>thee</u>tah el <u>loo</u>nes ah las <u>on</u>thay es<u>tah</u> byen

5 **Gracias, adiós.**
<u>gra</u>thyas, addy-<u>os</u>

2 On the phone

You are arranging an appointment. Follow the conversation, replying in Spanish following the English prompts.

Dígame, Apex Finanzas.
1 *I'd like to speak to Ana Flores.*

¿De parte de quién?
2 *Luis Cortés, of Don Frío.*

Lo siento, está comunicando.
3 *Can I leave a message?*

Sí, dígame.
4 *The appointment on Monday at 11am is fine.*

Muy bien, adiós.
5 *Thank you, goodbye.*

3 Clothing

Say the Spanish words for the numbered items of clothing.

tie ❶

jacket ❷

trousers ❸

❹ *skirt*

shoes ❺

tights ❻

3 Clothing

1 **la corbata**
lah kor<u>ba</u>tah

2 **la chaqueta**
lah cha<u>ke</u>tah

3 **el pantalón**
el panta<u>lon</u>

4 **la falda**
lah <u>fal</u>dah

5 **los zapatos**
los tha<u>pa</u>tos

6 **las medias**
las <u>me</u>deeas

4 At the doctor's

Say these phrases in Spanish.

1 *I don't feel well.*

2 *I have a heart condition.*

3 *Do I need to go to hospital?*

4 *I am pregnant.*

4 At the doctor's

1 **No me encuentro bien.**
noh may enk<u>wen</u>troh byen

2 **Tengo un problema de corazón.**
<u>ten</u>goh oon prob<u>le</u>mah day kora<u>thon</u>

3 **¿Necesito ir al hospital?**
nethe<u>see</u>toh eer al os<u>pee</u>tal

4 **Estoy embarazada.**
es<u>toy</u> embara<u>tha</u>dah

1 Warm up

Say the months of the year in Spanish. (pp.28–9)

Ask "Is there a car park?" and "Are there toilets?" (pp.48–9 and pp.62-3)

En casa
At home

Many city-dwellers live in apartment blocks (**edificios**), but in rural areas the houses tend to be detached (**chalet**). If you want to know how big it is you will need to ask in square metres. If you want to know how many bedrooms there are ask **¿Cuántos dormitorios hay?**.

2 Match and repeat

Match the numbered items to the list and test yourself using the flap.

1 **la chimenea**
lah cheemenayah

2 **la ventana**
lah bentanah

3 **el tejado**
el tehadoh

4 **la terraza**
lah terratha

5 **la persiana**
lah perseeanah

6 **el muro**
el mooroh

7 **la puerta**
lah pwertah

8 **el garaje**
el garahay

❶ chimney

❷ window

❻ wall

❺ shutters

Cultural tip You almost never see a Spanish home without shutters at every window. These are closed at night and often during the heat of the day in summer. Curtains, where they exist at all, tend to be more for decoration. Carpets are not popular in Spanish homes; ceramic tiles or parquet floors with rugs are a more common flooring solution.

3 Words to remember

Familiarize yourself with these words and test yourself using the flap.

¿**Cuánto es el alquiler al mes?**
kwantoh es el alkeeler al mes
What is the rent per month?

room	**la habitación** lah abeelathyon
floor	**el suelo** el sweloh
ceiling	**el techo** el techoh
bedroom	**el dormitorio** el dormeetoreeoh
bathroom	**el cuarto de baño** el kwartoh day banyoh
kitchen	**la cocina** lah kotheenah
dining room	**el comedor** el komedor
living room	**el cuarto de estar** el kwartoh day estar
cellar	**el sótano** el sotahnoh
attic	**el ático** el ahteekoh

3 *roof*

4 *terrace*

8 *garage*

7 *door*

4 Useful phrases

Practise these phrases and test yourself.

¿**Hay un garaje?**
ah-ee oon garahhay

Is there a garage?

¿**Cuándo está disponible?**
kwandoh estah deesponeeblay

When is it available?

¿**Está amueblado?**
estah amwebladoh

Is it furnished?

5 Say it

Is there a dining room?

Is it large?

Is it available in July?

1 Warm up

What is the Spanish for "table", "chair", "toilet(s)", and "curtains"? (pp.20–1, pp.80–1, pp.52–3, pp.60–1)

Say "beautiful", "soft", and "big". (pp.64–5)

En la casa
Inside the house

If you're renting a holiday house or villa in Spain, the most usual option is to take it for a full month or, if not, for a **quincena**, the first or last fifteen days of the month. You will need to check in advance whether the cost of utilities is included in the rent. Most holiday homes have no telephone.

2 Match and repeat

Match the numbered items to the list in the panel on the left. Then test yourself by concealing the Spanish with the cover flap.

① worktop

1 **la encimera**
lah enthee*mer*ah

2 **el fregadero**
el frega*der*oh

3 **el microondas**
el meekro-*on*das

4 **el horno**
el *or*noh

5 **la cocina**
lah ko*thee*nah

6 **el frigorífico**
el freego*ree*feekoh

7 **la mesa**
lah *mes*ah

8 **la silla**
lah *see*yah

⑤ cooker **⑥** fridge

④ oven

table **⑦**

3 In conversation

Este es el horno.
*es*tay es el *or*noh

This is the oven.

¿Hay también un lavavajillas?
ah-ee tamb*yen* oon lababa*hee*yas

Is there a dishwasher as well?

Sí, y hay un congelador grande.
see, ee ah-ee oon konhela*dor gran*day

Yes, and there's a big freezer.

4 Words to remember

Familiarize yourself with these words and test yourself using the flap.

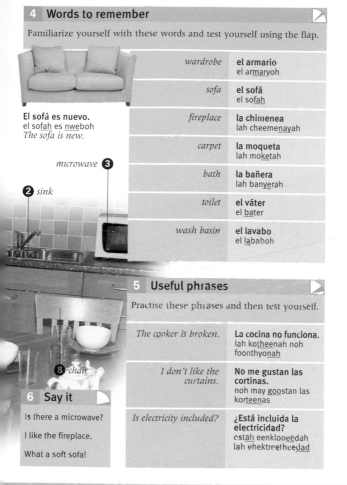

El sofá es nuevo.
el sofah es nweboh
The sofa is new.

wardrobe	**el armario**	el armaryoh
sofa	**el sofá**	el sofah
fireplace	**la chimenea**	lah cheemenayah
carpet	**la moqueta**	lah moketah
bath	**la bañera**	lah banyerah
toilet	**el váter**	el bater
wash basin	**el lavabo**	el lababoh

microwave ❸

❷ *sink*

❽ *chair*

5 Useful phrases

Practise these phrases and then test yourself.

The cooker is broken.	**La cocina no funciona.** lah kotheenah noh foonthyonah
I don't like the curtains.	**No me gustan las cortinas.** noh may goostan las korteenas
Is electricity included?	**¿Está incluida la electricidad?** estah eenklooeedah lah ehektreetheedad

6 Say it

Is there a microwave?

I like the fireplace.

What a soft sofa!

Todo está muy nuevo.
todoh estah mwee nweboh

Everything is very new.

Y aquí está la lavadora.
ee ahkee estah lah labadorah

And here is the washing machine.

¡Qué azulejos más bonitos!
kay ahthoolayhos mas boneetos

What beautiful tiles!

1 Warm up

Say "I need" and "you need". (pp.64–5, pp.92–4)

What is the Spanish for "day" and "month"? (pp.28–9)

Say the days of the week. (pp.28–9)

El jardín
The garden

The garden of a house or villa may be communal, or at least partly shared. Check with the estate agent or rental agent carefully to establish the position. In some cases, a charge for upkeep of the garden may be included with the rent of an apartment. Check with the agent.

2 Words to remember

Familiarize yourself with these words and test yourself using the flap.

la máquina cortacésped lah <u>make</u>enah korta<u>thes</u>ped	*lawn mower*
la horca lah <u>or</u>kah	*fork*
la pala lah <u>pa</u>lah	*spade*
el rastrillo el rra<u>stree</u>yoh	*rake*
el vivero el bee<u>ber</u>oh	*garden centre*

2 *tree*

3 *soil*

terrace **1**

flowers **7**   *weeds* **8**   **9** *path*

3 Useful phrases

Practise these phrases and then test yourself using the cover flap.

	The gardener comes once a week.	**El jardinero viene una vez a la semana.** el hardee<u>nai</u>roh <u>bya</u>inay <u>oo</u>nah beth ah lah se<u>ma</u>nah
	Can you mow the lawn?	**¿Puede cortar el césped?** <u>pwe</u>day kor<u>tar</u> el <u>thes</u>ped
	Is the garden private?	**¿Es el jardín privado?** es el har<u>deen</u> pree<u>ba</u>doh
	The garden needs watering	**El jardín necesita que lo rieguen.** el har<u>deen</u> nethe<u>see</u>tah kay loh rree<u>ay</u>ghen

4 Match and repeat

Match the numbered items to the words in the panel on the right.

4 *lawn* **5** *hedge* **6** *plants*

flowerbed **10**

1 **la terraza**
lah te<u>rra</u>thah

2 **el árbol**
el <u>ar</u>bol

3 **la tierra**
lah t<u>yai</u>rrah

4 **el césped**
el <u>thes</u>ped

5 **el seto**
el <u>se</u>toh

6 **las plantas**
las <u>plan</u>tas

7 **las flores**
las <u>flo</u>res

8 **las malas hierbas**
las <u>ma</u>las <u>yer</u>bas

9 **el camino**
el ka<u>mee</u>noh

10 **el parterre**
el par<u>tai</u>rray

5 Say it

The lawn needs water.

Are there any trees?

The gardener comes on Fridays.

Los animales de compañía
Pets

1 Warm up

Say "My name's …".
(pp.8–9)

Say "Don't worry".
(pp.94–5)

What's "your" in
Spanish? (pp.12–13)

"Pet passports" are now available to
enable holiday-makers and commuters
to take their pets with them to Spain
and avoid quarantine on return to the
UK. Consult your vet for details on the
necessary vaccinations and paperwork.

2 Match and repeat

Match the numbered animals to the Spanish
words in the panel on the left. Then test yourself
using the cover flap.

1 **el gato**
el gatoh

2 **el conejo**
el konehoh

3 **el pájaro**
el paharoh

4 **el pez**
el peth

5 **el perro**
el perroh

6 **el hámster**
el hamster

bird 3

2 rabbit

1 cat

fish 4

dog 5

6 hamster

3 Useful phrases

Learn these phrases and then test yourself using
the cover flap.

¿Es bueno el perro? es buenoh el perroh	*Is this dog friendly?*
¿Puedo llevar el perro? pwedoh yebar el perroh	*Can I bring my dog?*
Me dan miedo los gatos. may dan myaydoh los gatos	*I'm frightened of cats.*
Mi perro no muerde. mee perroh noh mweday	*My dog doesn't bite.*

Este gato está lleno de pulgas.
estay gatoh estah yenoh day poolgas
This cat is full of fleas.

Cultural tip Many dogs in Spain are working or guard dogs and you may encounter them tethered or roaming free. Approach farms and rural houses with particular care. Look out for warning notices such as "¡Cuidado con el perro!" (Beware of the dog).

¡CUIDADO CON EL PERRO!

4 Words to remember

Familiarize yourself with these words and test yourself using the flap.

Mi perro no está bien.
mee perroh noh est<u>uh</u> byen
My dog is not well

basket	**la cesta** lah <u>the</u>stah
cage	**la jaula** lah <u>hao</u>olah
bowl	**el bol** el bol
collar	**el collar** el k<u>o</u>yar
lead	**la correa** lah kor<u>ray</u>-ah
vet	**el veterinario** el betereen<u>a</u>ryoh
vaccination	**la vacuna** lah bak<u>oo</u>nah
pet passport	**el pasaporte de animales** el pasa<u>por</u>tay day anee<u>ma</u>les
flea spray	**el spray antipulgas** el es<u>prae</u>e anteepool<u>gas</u>

5 Put into practice

Join in this conversation. Read the Spanish on the left and follow the instructions to make your reply. Then test yourself by concealing the answers with the cover flap.

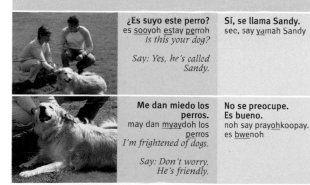

¿Es suyo este perro? es <u>soo</u>yoh <u>es</u>tay <u>pe</u>rroh *Is this your dog?* Say: Yes, he's called Sandy.	**Sí, se llama Sandy.** see, say <u>ya</u>mah Sandy
Me dan miedo los perros. may dan <u>myay</u>doh los <u>pe</u>rros *I'm frightened of dogs.* Say: Don't worry. He's friendly.	**No se preocupe. Es bueno.** noh say prayoh<u>koo</u>pay. es <u>bwe</u>noh

Respuestas
Answers
Cover with flap

Repase y repita
Review and repeat

1 Colours

Respuestas

1 **negra**
<u>ne</u>grah

2 **pequeños**
pe<u>ke</u>nyos

3 **rojo**
<u>rro</u>hoh

4 **verde**
<u>ber</u>day

5 **amarillos**
ama<u>ree</u>yos

1 Colours

Complete the sentences with the Spanish word for the colour in brackets. Watch out for masculine and feminine.

1 Quisiera la camisa _____. (black)

2 Estos zapatos son muy _____. (small)

3 ¿Tiene este traje en _____ ? (red)

4 No, pero lo tengo en _____. (green)

5 Quiero los zapatos _____. (yellow)

2 Kitchen

1 **la cocina**
lah ko<u>thee</u>nah

2 **el frigorífico**
el freego<u>ree</u>feekoh

3 **el fregadero**
el frega<u>de</u>roh

4 **el microondas**
el meekro-<u>on</u>das

5 **el horno**
el <u>or</u>noh

6 **la silla**
lah <u>see</u>yah

7 **la mesa**
lah <u>me</u>sah

2 Kitchen

Say the Spanish words for the numbered items.

❶ cooker

fridge ❷

oven ❺

chair ❻

3 House

You are visiting a house in Spain. Join in the conversation, asking questions in Spanish following the English prompts.

Éste es el cuarto de estar.
1 *What a lovely fireplace.*

Sí, y tiene una cocina muy grande.
2 *How many bedrooms are there?*

Hay tres dormitorios.
3 *Do you have a garage?*

Sí, pero no hay un jardín.
4 *When is it available?*

En julio.
5 *What is the rent a month?*

3 House

1 **¡Qué chimenea más bonita!**
kay cheemenayah mas boneetah

2 **¿Cuántos dormitorios hay?**
kwantos dormeetoreeos ah-ee

3 **¿Tiene garaje?**
tyenay garahay

4 **¿Cuándo está disponible?**
kwandoh estah deesponeeblay

5 **¿Cuánto es el alquiler al mes?**
kwantoh es el alkeeler al mes

microwave **4**

3 *sink*

table **7**

4 At home

Say the Spanish for the following items.

1 *washing machine*

2 *sofa*

3 *attic*

4 *dining room*

5 *tree*

6 *garden*

4 At home

1 **la lavadora**
lah labadorah

2 **el sofá**
el sofah

3 **el ático**
el ahteekoh

4 **el comedor**
el komedor

5 **el árbol**
el arbol

6 **el jardín**
el hardeen

1 Warm up

Ask "How do I get to the bank?" and "How do I get to the post office?" (pp.50–1)

What's the Spanish for "passport"? (pp.54–5)

How do you ask "What time is the meeting?" (pp.30–1)

El banco y la oficina de correos
Bank and post office

Banks and post offices usually open only until lunchtime (approximately 2pm) and are generally closed at weekends. **Cajas de ahorros** (savings banks) have different hours. In the summer opening times may be shorter.

2 Words to remember: post

Familiarize yourself with these words and test yourself using the cover flap to conceal the Spanish on the left.

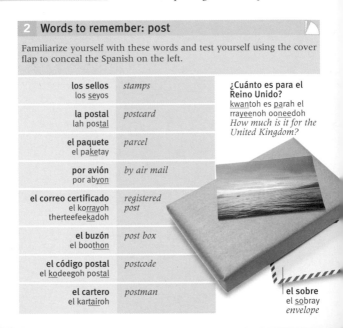

los sellos los <u>se</u>yos	*stamps*
la postal lah pos<u>tal</u>	*postcard*
el paquete el pa<u>ke</u>tay	*parcel*
por avión por ab<u>yon</u>	*by air mail*
el correo certificado el <u>ko</u>rrayoh therteefee<u>ka</u>doh	*registered post*
el buzón el boo<u>thon</u>	*post box*
el código postal el <u>ko</u>deegoh pos<u>tal</u>	*postcode*
el cartero el kar<u>tai</u>roh	*postman*

¿Cuánto es para el Reino Unido?
<u>kwan</u>toh es <u>pa</u>rah el rra<u>ye</u>enoh oo<u>nee</u>doh
How much is it for the United Kingdom?

el sobre
el <u>so</u>bray
envelope

3 In conversation

Quisiera sacar dinero.
kee<u>syai</u>rah sa<u>kar</u> dee<u>ne</u>roh

I'd like to withdraw some money.

¿Tiene identificación?
<u>tye</u>nay eedenteefeekath<u>yon</u>

Do you have any ID?

Sí, aquí tiene mi pasaporte.
see, ah<u>kee</u> <u>tye</u>nay mee pasa<u>por</u>tay

Yes, here's my passport.

4 Words to remember: bank

Familiarize yourself with these words and test yourself using the flap to cover the Spanish on the right.

PIN	**el pin** el peen
bank	**el banco** el bankoh
cashier	**el cajero** el kaheroh
cashpoint/ATM	**el cajero automático** el kaheroh aootomateekoh
notes	**los billetes** los beeyetes
travellers' cheques	**los cheques de viaje** los chekes day beeahay

¿Cómo puedo pagar?
komoh pwedoh pagar
How can I pay?

5 Useful phrases

Practise these phrases and then test yourself using the cover flap.

6 Say it

I'd like to change some travellers' cheques.

Do I need my passport?

I'd like a stamp for the United Kingdom.

I'd like to change some money.	**Quisiera cambiar dinero.** keesyairah kambyar deeneroh
What is the exchange rate?	**¿A cuánto está el cambio?** ah kwantoh estah el kambyoh
I'd like to withdraw some money.	**Quisiera sacar dinero.** keesyairah sakar deeneroh

Meta su pin, por favor.
metah soo peen, por fabor

Please key in your PIN.

¿Tengo que firmar también?
tengoh kay feermar tambyen

Do I have to sign as well?

No, no hace falta.
noh, noh ahthay faltah

No, that's not necessary.

What is the Spanish for "doesn't work"? (pp.60–1)

What's the Spanish for "today" and "tomorrow"? (pp.28–9)

Los servicios
Services

You can combine the Spanish words on these pages with the vocabulary you learned in week 10 to help you explain basic problems and cope with arranging most repairs. When organizing building work or a repair, it's a good idea to agree the price and method of payment in advance.

2 Words to remember

Familiarize yourself with these words and test yourself using the flap.

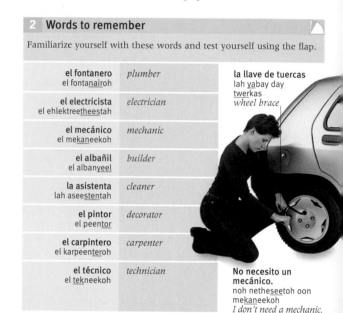

el fontanero el font<u>a</u>nairoh	*plumber*
el electricista el ehlektree<u>thees</u>tah	*electrician*
el mecánico el me<u>ka</u>neekoh	*mechanic*
el albañil el alban<u>yeel</u>	*builder*
la asistenta lah asee<u>sten</u>tah	*cleaner*
el pintor el peen<u>tor</u>	*decorator*
el carpintero el karpeen<u>ter</u>oh	*carpenter*
el técnico el <u>tek</u>neekoh	*technician*

la llave de tuercas
lah <u>ya</u>bay day <u>twer</u>kas
wheel brace

No necesito un mecánico.
noh nethe<u>see</u>toh oon me<u>ka</u>neekoh
I don't need a mechanic.

3 In conversation

La lavadora no funciona.
lah lab<u>a</u>dorah noh foothy<u>on</u>ah

The washing machine's not working.

Sí, la manguera está rota.
see, lah man<u>gher</u>ah estah <u>r</u>rotah

Yes, the hose is broken.

¿La puede arreglar?
lah <u>pwe</u>day arre<u>glar</u>

Can you repair it?

4 Useful phrases

Practise these phrases and then test yourself using the cover flap.

Can you clean the bathroom?	**¿Puede limpiar el cuarto de baño?** pweday leempyar el kwartoh day banyoh
Can you repair the boiler?	**¿Puede arreglar la caldera?** pweday arreglar lah kalderah
Do you know a good electrician?	**¿Conoce a un buen electricista?** konothay ah oon bwen ehlektreetheestah

¿Dónde me pueden arreglar la plancha?
donday may pweden arreglar lah planchah
Where can I get the iron repaired?`

5 Put into practice

Practise these phrases. Cover up the text on the right and complete the dialogue in Spanish. Check your answers and repeat if necessary.

los planos
los planos
plans

Su verja está rota.
soo berhah estah rrotah
Your gate is broken.

Ask: *Do you know a good builder?*

¿Conoce a un buen albañil?
konothay ah oon bwen albanyeel

Empiezo el trabajo mañana.
empyaythoh el trabahoh manyanah
I start the job tomorrow.

Sí, hay uno en el pueblo.
see, ah-ee oonoh en el pwebloh
Yes, there is one in the village.

Ask: *Do you have his phone number?*

¿Tiene su número de teléfono?
tyenay soo noomeroh day telefonoh

No, va a necesitar una nueva.
noh, bah ah netheseetar oonah nwebah

No, you'll need a new one.

¿Lo puede hacer hoy?
loh pweday ahther oy

Can you do it today?

No, volveré mañana.
noh, bolberay manyanah

No. I'll come back tomorrow.

1 Warm up

Say the days of the week in Spanish. (pp.28–9)

How do you say "cleaner"? (pp.110–11)

Say "It's 9.30", "10.45", "12.00". (pp.30–1)

Venir
To come

The verb **venir** (*to come*) is one of the most useful verbs. As well as the main verb (see below) it is worth knowing the instruction ¡**ven!**/¡**venga!** (*come here!* informal/formal). Note that *with me* becomes **conmigo** and *with you* **contigo**: **ven conmigo** (*come with me*); **vengo contigo** (*I'm going with you*).

2 Venir: to come

Say the different forms of the verb aloud, reading from the table. Use the cover flap to test yourself and, when you are confident, practise the sample sentences below.

yo vengo yoh <u>ben</u>goh	*I come*
tú vienes/usted viene too <u>bye</u>nes/<u>oos</u>ted <u>bye</u>nay	*you come (informal/ formal singular)*
él/ella viene el/<u>eh</u>-yah <u>bye</u>nay	*he/she comes*
nosotros(-as) venimos no<u>so</u>tros(-as) be<u>nee</u>mos	*we come*
vosotros(-as) venís bo<u>so</u>tros(-as) be<u>nees</u>	*you come (informal plural)*
ustedes vienen oos<u>te</u>des <u>bye</u>nen	*you come (formal plural)*
ellos/ellas vienen <u>eh</u>-yos/<u>eh</u>-yas <u>bye</u>nen	*they come*
Vengo ahora. <u>ben</u>goh ah-<u>o</u>rah	*I'm coming now.*
Venimos todos los martes. be<u>nee</u>mos <u>to</u>dos los <u>mar</u>tes	*We come every Tuesday.*
Vienen en tren. <u>bye</u>nen en tren	*They come by train.*

Vienen en muchos colores.
bee<u>ay</u>nen en <u>moo</u>chos <u>ko</u>lores
They come in many colours.

Conversational tip To say "I come from England" in Spanish, you have to use the verb "to be", as in "soy inglés" (I am from England). When you use the verb "to come", as in "Vengo de Londres", it means you have just arrived from London.

3 Useful phrases

Learn these phrases and then test yourself using the cover flap.

When can I come?	**¿Cuándo puedo venir?** kwandoh pwedoh beneer
Does it come in size 44?	**¿Viene en la talla 44?** byenay en lah tayah kwarentah ee kwatroh
The cleaner comes every Monday.	**La asistenta viene todos los lunes.** lah aseestentah byenay todos los loones
Come with me. (informal/formal)	**Ven conmigo/ Venga conmigo.** ben konmeegoh/ bengah konmeegoh

¿Puede venir el viernes?
pweday beneer el byairnes
Can you come on Friday?

4 Put into practice

Practise these phrases. Then cover up the text on the right and say the answering part of the dialogue in Spanish. Check your answers and repeat if necessary.

Peluquería Cristina, dígame.
pelookereeah kristeenah, deegamay
Christine's hair salon. Can I help you?

Say: I'd like an appointment.

Quisiera una cita.
keesyairah oonah theetah

¿Cuándo quiere venir?
kwandoh kyairay beneer
When do you want to come?

Say: Today, if possible.

Hoy, si es posible.
oy, see es poseeblay

Sí, claro. ¿A qué hora?
see klaroh, ah kay orah
Yes of course. What time?

Say: At 10.30.

A las diez y media.
ah las dyeth ee medeeah

La policía y el delito
Police and crime

1 Warm up

What's the Spanish for "big" and "small"? (pp.64–5)

Say "The room is big" and "The bed is small". (pp.64–5)

While in Spain, if you are the victim of a crime, you should go to the police station to report it, or in an emergency you can dial 112. You may have to explain your complaint in Spanish, so some basic vocabulary is useful.

2 Words to remember: crime

Familiarize yourself with these words.

el robo el rroboh	*robbery*
la denuncia lah denoontheeah	*police report*
el ladrón el ladron	*thief*
la policía lah poleetheeah	*police*
la declaración lah deklarathyon	*statement*
el testigo el testeegoh	*witness*
el abogado el abogadoh	*lawyer*

Necesito un abogado.
 netheseetoh oon abogadoh
 I need a lawyer.

3 Useful phrases

Learn these phrases and then test yourself.

Me han robado. may an rrobadoh	*I've been robbed.*
¿Qué han robado? kay an rrobadoh	*What was stolen?*
¿Vió quién lo hizo? byoh kyain loh eethoh	*Did you see who did it?*
¿Cuándo ocurrió? kwandoh okoorryoh	*When did it happen?*

la cámara de fotos
 lah kamarah day fotos
 camera

la cartera
 la karterah
 purse

4 Words to remember: appearance

Learn these words. Remember some adjectives have a feminine form.

Él es bajo y tiene bigote.
el es bahoh ee tyenay beegotay
He is short and has a moustache.

Tiene el pelo negro y corto.
tyenay el peloh negroh ee kortoh
He has short, black hair.

man	**el hombre** el ombray	
woman	**la mujer** lah moo-hair	
tall	**alto/alta** altoh/altah	
short	**bajo/baja** bahoh/bahah	
young	**joven** hoben	
old	**viejo/vieja** byayhoh/byayhah	
fat	**gordo/gorda** gordoh/gordah	
thin	**delgado/delgada** delgadoh/delgadah	
long/short hair	**el pelo largo/corto** el peloh largoh/kortoh	
glasses	**las gafas** las gafas	
beard	**la barba** la barbah	

Cultural tip In Spain there is a difference between la guardia civil and la policía. La policía are the local police while la guardia civil operates in airports and patrols the national road system. The police uniforms are blue and those of the guardia civil are green.

5 Put into practice

Practise these phrases. Then cover up the text on the right and follow the instructions to make your reply in Spanish.

¿Cómo era? komoh ehrah *What did he look like?* Say: Short and fat.	**Bajo y gordo.** bahoh ee gordoh
¿Y el pelo? ee el peloh *And his hair?* Say: Long with a beard.	**Largo y con barba.** largoh ee kon barbah

Repase y repita
Review and repeat

Respuestas
Answers
Cover with flap

1 To come

1 **vienen**
<u>bye</u>nen

2 **viene**
<u>bye</u>nay

3 **venimos**
ben<u>ee</u>mos

4 **venís**
ben<u>ees</u>

5 **vengo**
<u>ben</u>goh

1 To come

Put the correct form of **venir** (*to come*) into the gaps.

1 Mis padres _____ a las cuatro.

2 La asistenta _____ una vez a la semana.

3 Nosotros _____ todos los martes.

4 ¿ _____ vosotros con nosotros?

5 Yo _____ en taxi.

2 Bank and post

1 **los billetes**
los bee<u>ye</u>tes

2 **la postal**
lah pos<u>tal</u>

3 **el paquete**
el pa<u>ke</u>tay

4 **el sobre**
el <u>so</u>bray

2 Bank and post

Name these items.

1 *notes*

2 *postcard*

3 *parcel*

4 *envelope*

3 Appearance

What do these descriptions mean?

1 Es un hombre alto y delgado.

2 Ella tiene el pelo corto y gafas.

3 Soy baja y tengo el pelo largo.

4 Ella es vieja y gorda.

5 Él tiene los ojos azules y barba.

3 Appearance

1 *He's a tall thin man.*

2 *She has short hair and glasses.*

3 *I'm short and I have long hair.*

4 *She's old and fat.*

5 *He has blue eyes and a beard.*

4 The pharmacy

You are asking a pharmacist for advice. Join in the conversation, replying in Spanish following the English prompts.

Buenos días, ¿qué desea?
1 *I have a cough.*

¿Le duele el pecho?
2 *No, but I have a headache.*

Tiene estas pastillas.
3 *Do you have that as a syrup?*

Sí señor. Aquí tiene.
4 *Thank you. How much is that?*

Cuatro euros.
5 *Here you are. Goodbye.*

4 The pharmacy

1 **Tengo tos.**
tengoh tos

2 **No, pero me duele la cabeza.**
noh, peroh may dwelay lah kabethah

3 **¿Lo tiene en jarabe?**
loh tyenay en harabay

4 **Gracias. ¿Cuánto es?**
grathyas. kwantoh es

5 **Aquí tiene. Adiós.**
ahkee tyenay. addy-os

1 Warm up

What is the Spanish for "museum" and "art gallery"? (pp.48–9)

Say "I don't like the curtains". (pp.100–1)

Ask "Do you want…?" informally. (pp.22–3)

El ocio
Leisure time

The Spanish pride themselves on their lively nightlife and support for the arts, including theatre and film. It is not unusual for Spaniards to number politics or philosophy among their interests. Be prepared for these topics to be the subject of conversation in social situations.

2 Words to remember

Familiarize yourself with these words and test yourself using the cover flap to conceal the Spanish on the left.

el teatro el te-ahtroh	*theatre*
el cine el theenay	*cinema*
la discoteca lah deeskotekah	*discotheque*
el deporte el deportay	*sport*
el turismo el tooreesmoh	*sightseeing*
la política la poleeteekah	*politics*
la música lah mooseekah	*music*
el arte el artay	*art*

Me encanta el baile.
me enkantah el baeelay
I love dancing.

3 In conversation

Hola. ¿Quieres jugar al tenis hoy?
o-lah. kyaires hoogar al tenis oy

Hi, do you want to play tennis today?

No, no me gusta el deporte.
noh, noh may goostah el deportay

No, I don't like sport.

Y entonces, ¿qué te gusta?
ee entonthes, kay tay goostah

So then, what do you like?

4 Useful phrases

Learn these phrases and then test yourself using the cover flap.

What are your (formal/informal) interests?	**¿Cuáles son sus/tus intereses?** kwales son soos/toos intereses
I like the theatre.	**Me gusta el teatro.** may goostah el te-ahtroh
I prefer the cinema.	**Yo prefiero el cine.** yoh prefyairoh el theenay
I'm interested in art.	**Me interesa el arte.** may interesah el artay
That bores me	**Eso me aburre.** ehsoh may aboorray

los video-juegos
los beedayoh-hwegos
video games

la bailadora
lah baeeladorah
dancer

el traje típico
el trahay teepeekoh
traditional costume

5 Say It

I'm interested in music.

I prefer sport.

I don't like video games.

Prefiero el turismo e ir de compras.
prefyairoh el tooreesmoh eh eer day kompras

I prefer sightseeing and shopping.

Eso a mí no me interesa.
ehsoh ah mee noh may interesah

That doesn't interest me.

No pasa nada. Me voy yo sola.
noh pasah nadah. may boy yoh solah

No problem. I'll go on my own.

1 Warm up

Ask "Do you (formal) want to play tennis?" (pp.118–19)

Say "I like the theatre" and "I prefer sightseeing". (pp.118–19)

Say "That doesn't interest me". (pp.118–19)

El deporte y los pasatiempos
Sport and hobbies

Hacer (*to do* or *to make*) and **jugar** (*to play*) are the verbs used most when talking about sport and pastimes. **Jugar** is followed by **a** when you are talking about playing a sport, as in **juego al baloncesto** (*I play basketball*).

2 Words to remember

Familiarize yourself with these words and then test yourself.

el fútbol/rugby el <u>foot</u>bol/<u>roog</u>bee	*football/rugby*
el tenis/baloncesto el <u>ten</u>is/balon<u>thes</u>toh	*tennis/basketball*
la natación lah natath<u>yon</u>	*swimming*
la vela lah <u>be</u>lah	*sailing*
la pesca lah <u>pes</u>kah	*fishing*
la pintura lah peen<u>too</u>rah	*painting*
el ciclismo el thee<u>klees</u>moh	*cycling*
el senderismo el sende<u>rees</u>moh	*hiking*

el búnker
 el <u>bun</u>ker
 bunker

el jugador de golf
 el <u>hu</u>gador day golf
 golfer

Juego al golf todos los días.
 <u>hwe</u>goh al golf todos los <u>dee</u>yas
 I play golf every day.

3 Useful phrases

Learn these phrases and then test yourself.

Juego al fútbol. <u>hwe</u>goh al <u>foot</u>bol	*I play football.*
Juega al tenis. <u>hwe</u>gah al <u>ten</u>is	*He plays tennis.*
Ella pinta. eh-yah <u>peen</u>tah	*She paints.*

4 Hacer: to do or to make

Hacer is a useful verb meaning "to do" or "to make". It is commonly used to describe leisure pursuits. **Hace** is also used to describe the weather.

Hoy hace bueno.
oy ahthay bwenoh
It's nice (weather) today.

la banderola
lah bandairolah
flag

el campo de golf
el kampoh day golf
golf course

I do	**yo hago** yoh ahgoh
you do (informal/formal singular)	**tú haces/usted hace** too ahthes/oosted ahthay
he/she does	**él/ella hace** el/eh-yah ahthay
we do	**nosotros(-as) hacemos** nosotros(-as) ahthemos
you do (informal plural)	**vosotros(-as) hacéis** bosotros(-as) ahthays
you do (formal plural)	**ustedes hacen** oostedes ahthen
they do	**ellos/ellas hacen** eh-yos/eh-yas ahthen
What do you like doing? (informal/formal singular)	**¿Qué te/le gusta hacer?** kay tay/lay goostah ahthair?
I go hiking.	**Yo hago senderismo.** yoh ahgoh sendereesmoh

5 Put into practice

Join in this conversation following the English prompts.

¿Qué te gusta hacer? kay tay goostah ahthair *What do you like doing?* Say: *I like playing tennis.*	**Me gusta jugar al tenis.** may goostah hoogar al tenis
¿Juegas al fútbol también? hwegas al footbol tambyen *Do you play football as well?* Say: *No, I play rugby.*	**No, juego al rugby.** noh, hwegoh al roogbee
¿Cuándo juegas? kwandoh hwegas *When do you play?* Say: *I play every week.*	**Juego todas las semanas.** hwegoh todas las semanas

La vida social
Socializing

1 Warm up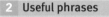

Say "my husband" and "my wife". (pp.10–11)

Say the days of the week in Spanish. (pp.28–9)

Say "Sorry, I'm busy". (pp.32–3)

The Spanish dinner table is the centre of the social world. You can expect to do a lot of your socializing around the table, enjoying food and wine. In general it is best to use the more polite **usted** form to talk to older people and **tú** with the younger crowd.

2 Useful phrases

Practise these phrases and then test yourself.

Me gustaría invitarte a cenar. may goostar<u>ee</u>ah inbeet<u>ar</u>tay ah the<u>nar</u>	*I'd like to invite you to dinner.*
¿Estás libre el miércoles que viene? estas <u>lee</u>bray el my<u>air</u>koles kay <u>byen</u>ay	*Are you free next Wednesday?*
Quizá otro día. keet<u>hah</u> <u>oh</u>troh <u>dee</u>yah	*Perhaps another day.*

Cultural tip When you visit someone's house for the first time, it is usual to bring flowers or wine. If you are invited again, having seen your host's house, you can bring something a little more personal.

3 In conversation

¿Quieres venir a comer el martes?
<u>kyaires</u> be<u>neer</u> ah ko<u>mer</u> el <u>mar</u>tes

Would you like to come to lunch on Tuesday?

Lo siento, estoy ocupada.
loh <u>syain</u>toh, estoy okoo<u>pa</u>dah

I'm sorry, I'm busy.

¿Qué tal el jueves?
kay tal el <u>hwe</u>bes

What about Thursday?

4 Words to remember

Familiarize yourself with these words and test yourself using the flap.

la invitada
lah inbeetadah
guest

la anfitriona
lah anfeetryonah
hostess

party	**la fiesta** lah fyaystah
dinner party	**la cena** lah thenah
invitation	**la invitación** lah inbeetathyon
reception	**la recepción** lah rrethepthyon
cocktail party	**el coctel** el koktel

5 Put into practice

Join this conversation, replying in Spanish.

¿Puede venir a una recepción esta noche?
pweday beneer ah oonah rrethepthyon estah nochay
Can you come to a reception tonight?

Say: Yes, I'd love to.

Sí, encantado/-a.
see, enkan-tadoh/-ah

Empieza a las ocho.
empyaythah ah las ochoh
It starts at eight o'clock.

Ask: What should I wear?

¿Qué me pongo?
kay may pongoh

Gracias por invitarnos.
grathyas por inbeetarnos
Thank you for inviting us.

Encantada.
enkan-tadah

I'd be delighted.

Ven con tu marido.
ben kon too mareedoh

Bring your husband.

Gracias, ¿a qué hora?
grathyas, ah kay orah

Thank you, at what time?

Respuestas
Answers
Cover with flap

Repase y repita
Review and repeat

1 Animals

1 **el pez**
   el peth

2 **el pájaro**
   el paharoh

3 **el conejo**
   el konehoh

4 **el gato**
   el gatoh

5 **el hámster**
   el hamster

6 **el perro**
   el perroh

1 Animals

Name the numbered animals in Spanish.

② bird

⑤ hamster

① fish

④ cat

2 I like...

1 **Me gusta el
   fútbol.**
   may goostah el
   footbol

2 **No me gusta el
   golf.**
   noh may goostah
   el golf

3 **Me gusta pintar.**
   may goostah
   peentar

4 **No me gustan las
   flores.**
   noh may goostan
   las flores

2 I like...

Say the following in Spanish:

1 *I like football.*

2 *I don't like golf.*

3 *I like painting.*

4 *I don't like flowers.*

3 rabbit

6 dog

3 Hacer

Use the correct form of the verb **hacer** (*to do* or *to make*) in these sentences.

1 Vosotros _____ senderismo.

2 Ella _____ eso todos los días.

3 ¿Qué _____ tú?

4 Hoy no _____ frío.

5 ¿Qué _____ ellos esta noche?

6 Yo _____ natación.

3 Hacer

1 **hacéis**
ah<u>thays</u>

2 **hace**
<u>ah</u>thay

3 **haces**
<u>ah</u>thes

4 **hace**
<u>ah</u>thay

5 **hacen**
<u>ah</u>then

6 **hago**
<u>ah</u>goh

4 An invitation

You are invited for dinner. Join in the conversation, replying in Spanish following the English prompts.

¿Quieres venir a comer el viernes?
1 *I'm sorry, I'm busy.*

¿Qué tal el sábado?
2 *I'd be delighted.*

Ven con los niños.
3 *Thank you. What time?*

A las doce y media.
4 *That's good for me.*

4 An invitation

1 **Lo siento, estoy ocupado/-a.**
loh <u>syen</u>toh, es<u>toy</u> okoo<u>pa</u>doh/-ah

2 **Encantado/-a.**
enkan-<u>ta</u>doh/-ah

3 **Gracias. ¿A qué hora?**
<u>grath</u>yas. ah kay <u>o</u>rah

4 **Me viene bien.**
may <u>byen</u>ay byen

Reinforce and progress

Regular practice is the key to maintaining and advancing your language skills. In this section you will find a variety of suggestions for reinforcing and extending your knowledge of Spanish. Many involve returning to exercises in the book and using the dictionaries to extend their scope. Go back through the lessons in a different order, mix and match activities to make up your own 15-minute daily programme, or focus on topics that are of particular relevance to your current needs.

Keep warmed up
Re-visit the Warm Up boxes to remind yourself of key words and phrases. Make sure you work your way through all of them on a regular basis.

1 Warm up

Say "I'm sorry"?
(pp.32–3)

What is the Spanish for "I'd like an appointment".
(pp.22–3 and pp.32–3)

How do you say "when?" in Spanish?
(pp.32–3)

2 I'd like...

Say "I'd like" the following:

churros ②   sugar ③

❶ black coffee

white coffee ❹

Review and repeat again
Work through a Review and Repeat lesson as a way of reinforcing words and phrases presented in the course. Return to the main lesson for any topic on which you are no longer confident.

3 In conversation: taxi

Carry on conversing
Re-read the In Conversation panels. Say both parts of the conversation, paying attention to the pronunciation. Where possible, try incorporating new words from the dictionary.

A la Plaza de España, por favor.
ah lah plathah day espanyah, por fabor

Plaza de España, please.

Sí, de acuerdo, señor.
see, day akwairdo, senyor

Yes, certainly, sir.

¿Me puede dejar ac| por favor?
may pweday dehar ahkee, por fabor

Can you drop me he| please?

4 Useful phrases

Learn these phrases and then test yourself using the cover flap.

ABIERTO OPEN	What time do you open/close?	¿A qué hora abre/cierra? ah kay orah <u>ah</u>bray/thy<u>ai</u>rrah
	Where are the toilets?	¿Dónde están los servicios? donday estan los ser<u>beeth</u>yos
	Is there access for wheelchairs?	¿Hay acceso para sillas de ruedas? ah-ee ak<u>thes</u>oh parah <u>see</u>yas day <u>rwe</u>das

Practise phrases
Return to the Useful Phrases and Put into Practice exercises. Test yourself using the cover flap. When you are confident, devise your own versions of the phrases, using new words from the dictionary.

Match, repeat, and extend
Remind yourself of words related to specific topics by returning to the Match and Repeat and Words to Remember exercises. Test yourself using the cover flap. Discover new words in that area by referring to the dictionary and menu guide.

2 *beans*

3 *mushrooms*

4 *grapes*

5 Match and repeat

Match the numbered items in this scene with the text in the panel.

1	los tomates	los to<u>ma</u>tes
2	las judías	las hoo<u>dee</u>as
3	los champiñones	los champee<u>nyo</u>nes
4	las uvas	las <u>oo</u>bas
5	los pepinos	los pe<u>pee</u>nos
6	las alcachofas	las alka<u>cho</u>fas
7	los guisantes	los ghee<u>san</u>tes
8	los pimientos	los peem<u>yain</u>tos

1 *tomatoes*

6 *cucumbers*

peas **7**

artichokes **6**

peppers **8**

Say it again
The Say It execises are a useful instant reminder for each lesson. Practise these, using your own vocabulary variations from the dictionary or elsewhere in the lesson.

6 Say it

The lawn needs watering.

Are there any trees?

The gardener comes on Fridays.

Using other resources

In addition to working with this book, try the following language extension ideas:

- Visit a Spanish-speaking country and try out your new skills with native speakers. Find out if there is a Spanish community near you. There may be shops, cafés, restaurants, and clubs. Try to visit some of these and use your Spanish to order food and drink and strike up conversations. Most native speakers will be happy to speak Spanish to you.

- Join a language class or club. There are usually evening and day classes available at a variety of different levels. Or you could start a club yourself if you have friends who are also interested in keeping up their Spanish.

- Look at Spanish magazines and newspapers. The pictures will help you to understand the text. Advertisements are also a useful way of expanding your vocabulary.

- Use the Internet, where you can find all kinds of websites for learning languages, some of which offer free online help and activities. You can also find Spanish websites for everything from renting a house to shampooing your pet. You can even access Spanish radio and TV stations online. Start by going to a Spanish search engine, such as *ozu.es*, and keying a hobby or sport that interests you, or set yourself a challenge, such as finding a two-bedroom house for rent in Madrid.

Menu guide

This guide lists the most common terms you may encounter on Spanish menus or when shopping for food. If you can't find an exact phrase, try looking up its component parts.

A

aceitunas *olives*
acelgas *spinach beet*
achicoria *chicory*
aguacate *avocado*
ahumados *smoked*
agua mineral *mineral water*
ajo *garlic*
al ajillo *with garlic*
a la parrilla *grilled*
a la plancha *grilled*
albaricoques *apricots*
albóndigas *meatballs*
alcachofas *artichokes*
alcaparras *capers*
al horno *baked*
allioli *garlic mayonnaise*
almejas *clams*
almejas a la marinera *clams stewed in wine and parsley*
almejas naturales *live clams*
almendras *almonds*
almíbar *syrup*
alubias *beans*
ancas de rana *frogs' legs*
anchoas *anchovies*
anguila *eel*
angulas *baby eels*
arenque *herring*
arroz a la cubana *rice with fried eggs and banana fritters*
arroz a la valenciana *rice with seafood*
arroz con leche *rice pudding*
asados *roast meat*
atún *tuna*
azúcar *sugar*

B

bacalao a la vizcaína *cod served with ham, peppers, and chillies*
bacalao al pil pil *cod served with chillies and garlic*
batido *milk shake*
bebidas *drinks*
berenjenas *aubergine*
besugo al horno *baked sea bream*
bistec de ternera *veal steak*
bonito *fish similar to tuna*

boquerones fritos *fried fresh anchovies*
brazo gitano *swiss roll*
brocheta de riñones *kidney kebabs*
buñuelos *fried pastries*
butifarra *Catalan sausage*

C

cabrito asado *roast kid*
cacahuetes *peanuts*
cachelada *pork stew with eggs, tomato, and onion*
café *coffee*
café con leche *coffee with steamed milk*
calabacines *courgette*
calabaza *pumpkin*
calamares a la romana *squid rings in batter*
calamares en su tinta *squid cooked in their ink*
caldeirada *fish soup*
caldereta gallega *vegetable stew*
caldo de ... ... *soup*
caldo de gallina *chicken soup*
caldo de pescado *clear fish soup*
caldo gallego *vegetable soup*
caldo guanche *soup of potatoes, tomatoes, onions, and courgettes*
callos a la madrileña *tripe cooked with chillies*
camarones *baby prawns*
canela *cinnamon*
cangrejos *crabs*
caracoles *snails*
caramelos *sweets*
carnes *meats*
castañas *chestnuts*
cebolla *onion*
cebolletas *spring onions*
centollo *spider crab*
cerdo *pork*
cerezas *cherries*
cerveza *beer*
cesta de frutas *selection of fresh fruit*
champiñones *mushrooms*
chanquetes *fish (similar to whitebait)*
chipirones *baby squid*
chipirones en su tinta *squid cooked in their ink*
chocos *cuttlefish*

chorizo *spicy sausage*
chuleta de buey *beef chop*
chuleta de cerdo *pork chop*
chuleta de cerdo empanada *breaded pork chop*
chuleta de cordero *lamb chop*
chuleta de cordero empanada *breaded lamb chop*
chuleta de ternera *veal chop*
chuleta de ternera empanada *breaded veal chop*
chuletas de lomo ahumado *smoked pork chops*
chuletitas de cordero *small lamb chops*
chuletón *large chop*
chuletón de buey *large beef chop*
churros *deep-fried pastry strips*
cigalas *crayfish*
cigalas cocidas *boiled crayfish*
ciruelas *plums*
ciruelas pasas *prunes*
cochinillo asado *roast suckling pig*
cocido *meat, chickpea, and vegetable stew*
cocktail de bogavante *lobster cocktail*
cocochas (de merluza) *hake stew*
cóctel de gambas *prawn cocktail*
cóctel de langostinos *jumbo prawn cocktail*
cóctel de mariscos *seafood cocktail*
codornices *quail*
codornices escabechadas *marinated quail*
codornices estofadas *braised quail*
col *cabbage*
coles de Bruselas *Brussels sprouts*
coliflor *cauliflower*
coñac *brandy*
conejo *rabbit*
conejo encebollado *rabbit with onions*
congrio *conger eel*

consomé con yema *consommé with egg yolk*
consomé de ave *fowl consommé*
contra de ternera con guisantes *veal stew with peas*
contrafilete de ternera *veal fillet*
copa *glass (of wine)*
copa de helado *ice cream, assorted flavours*
cordero asado *roast lamb*
cordero chilindrón *lamb stew with onion, tomato, peppers, and eggs*
costillas de cerdo *pork ribs*
crema catalana *crème brûlée*
cremada *dessert made with egg, sugar, and milk*
crema de... *cream of ... soup*
crema de legumbres *cream of vegetable soup*
crepe imperiale *crêpe suzette*
criadillas de tierra *truffles*
crocante *ice cream with chopped nuts*
croquetas *croquettes*
cuajada *curds*

D, E

dátiles *dates*
embutidos *sausages*
embutidos de la tierra *local sausages*
empanada gallega *fish pie*
empanada santiaguesa *fish pie*
empanadillas *small pies*
endivia *endive*
en escabeche *marinated*
ensalada *salad*
ensalada de arenque *fish salad*
ensalada ilustrada *mixed salad*
ensalada mixta *mixed salad*
ensalada simple *green salad*
ensaladilla rusa *Russian salad (potatoes, carrots, peas, and other vegetables in mayonnaise)*
entrecot a la parrilla *grilled entrecôte*
entremeses *hors d'oeuvres, starters*
escalope a la milanesa *breaded veal with cheese*
escalope a la parrilla *grilled veal*
escalope a la plancha *grilled veal*
escalope de lomo de cerdo *escalope of pork fillet*

escalope de ternera *veal escalope*
escalope empanado *breaded escalope*
escalopines al vino de Marsala *veal escalopes cooked in Marsala wine*
escalopines de ternera *veal escalopes*
espadín a la toledana *kebab*
espaguetis *spaghetti*
espárragos *asparagus*
espárragos trigueros *wild green asparagus*
espinacas *spinach*
espinazo de cerdo con patatas *stew of pork ribs with potatoes*
estofado *braised; stew*
estragón *tarragon*

F

fabada (asturiana) *bean stew with sausage*
faisán *pheasant*
faisán trufado *pheasant with truffles*
fiambres *cold meats*
fideos *thin pasta, noodles*
filete a la parrilla *grilled beef steak*
filete de cerdo *pork steak*
filete de ternera *veal steak*
flan *crème caramel*
frambuesas *raspberries*
fresas *strawberries*
fritos *fried*
fruta *fruit*

G

gallina en pepitoria *chicken stew with peppers*
gambas *prawns*
gambas cocidas *boiled prawns*
gambas en gabardina *prawns in batter*
gambas rebozadas *prawns in batter*
garbanzos *chickpeas*
garbanzos a la catalana *chickpeas with sausage, boiled eggs, and pine nuts*
gazpacho andaluz *cold tomato soup*
gelatina de ... ... *jelly*
gratén de ... ... *au gratin (baked in a cream and cheese sauce)*
granizada *crushed ice drink*
gratinada/o *au gratin*
grelo *turnip*
grillado *grilled*
guisantes *peas*
guisantes salteados *sautéed peas*

H

habas *broad beans*
habichuelas *white beans*
helado *ice cream*
helado de vainilla *vanilla ice cream*
helado de turrón *nougat ice cream*
hígado *liver*
hígado de ternera *calves' liver*
hígado estofado *braised liver*
higos con miel y nueces *figs with honey and nuts*
higos secos *dried figs*
horchata (de chufas) *cold drink made from chufa nuts*
huevo hilado *egg yolk garnish*
huevos *eggs*
huevos a la flamenca *fried eggs with ham, tomato, and vegetables*
huevos cocidos *hard-boiled eggs*
huevos con patatas fritas *fried eggs and chips*
huevos con picadillo *eggs with minced meat*
huevos duros *hard-boiled eggs*
huevos escalfados *poached eggs*
huevos pasados por agua *soft-boiled eggs*
huevos revueltos *scrambled eggs*

J

jamón *ham*
jamón con huevo hilado *ham with egg yolk garnish*
jamón serrano *cured ham*
jarra de vino *wine jug*
jerez *sherry*
jeta *pigs' cheeks*
judías verdes *green beans*
judías verdes a la española *bean stew*
judías verdes al natural *plain green beans*
jugo de ... ... *juice*

L

langosta *lobster*
langosta a la americana *lobster with brandy and garlic*
langosta a la catalana *lobster with mushrooms and ham in white sauce*
langosta fría con mayonesa *cold lobster with mayonnaise*

langostinos *king prawns*
langostinos dos salsas *king prawns cooked in two sauces*
laurel *bay leaves*
leche *milk*
leche frita *pudding made from milk and eggs*
leche merengada *cold milk with meringue*
lechuga *lettuce*
lengua de buey *ox tongue*
lengua de cordero *lambs' tongue*
lenguado a la romana *sole in batter*
lenguado meuniere *sole meunière (floured sole fried in butter)*
lentejas *lentils*
lentejas aliñadas *lentils in vinaigrette dressing*
licores *spirits, liqueurs*
liebre estofada *stewed hare*
lima *lime*
limón *lemon*
lombarda *red cabbage*
lomo curado *pork loin sausage*
lonchas de jamón *sliced, cured ham*
longaniza *cooked Spanish sausage*
lubina *sea bass*
lubina a la marinera *sea bass in a parsley sauce*

M

macedonia de fruta *fruit salad*
mahonesa *or* mayonesa *mayonnaise*
Málaga *a sweet wine*
mandarinas *tangerines*
manitas de cordero *lamb shank*
manos de cerdo *pigs' feet*
manos de cerdo a la parrilla *grilled pigs' feet*
mantecadas *small sponge cakes*
mantequilla *butter*
manzanas *apples*
mariscada *cold mixed shellfish*
mariscos del día *fresh shellfish*
mariscos del tiempo *seasonal shellfish*
medallones *steaks*
media de agua *half bottle of mineral water*
mejillones *mussels*
mejillones a la marinera *mussels in a wine sauce*
melocotón *peach*
melón *melon*
menestra de legumbres *vegetable stew*

menú de la casa *set menu*
menú del día *set menu*
merluza *hake*
merluza a la cazuela *stewed hake*
merluza al ajo arriero *hake with garlic and chillies*
merluza a la riojana *hake with chillies*
merluza a la romana *hake steaks in batter*
merluza a la vasca *hake in a garlic sauce*
merluza en salsa *hake in sauce*
merluza en salsa verde *hake in a green (parsley and wine) sauce*
merluza fría *cold hake*
merluza frita *fried hake*
mermelada *jam*
mero *grouper (fish)*
mero en salsa verde *grouper in green (garlic and parsley) sauce*
mollejas de ternera fritas *fried sweetbreads*
morcilla *blood sausage*
morcilla de carnero *mutton blood sausage*
morros de cerdo *pigs' cheeks*
morros de vaca *cows' cheeks*
mortadela *salami-type sausage*
morteruelo *kind of pâté*

N, O

nabo *turnip*
naranjas *oranges*
nata *cream*
natillas *cold custard*
níscalos *wild mushrooms*
nueces *walnuts*
orejas de cerdo *pigs' ears*

P

paella *fried rice with seafood and/or meat*
paella castellana *meat paella*
paella valenciana *shellfish, rabbit, and chicken paella*
paleta de cordero lechal *shoulder of lamb*
pan *bread*
panache de verduras *vegetable stew*
panceta *bacon*
parrillada de caza *mixed grilled game*
parrillada de mariscos *mixed grilled shellfish*
pasas *raisins*
pastel de ternera *veal pie*
pasteles *cakes*

patatas a la pescadora *potatoes with fish*
patatas asadas *baked potatoes*
patatas bravas *potatoes in spicy tomato sauce*
patatas fritas *chips*
patitos rellenos *stuffed duckling*
pato a la naranja *duck in orange sauce*
pavo *turkey*
pavo trufado *turkey stuffed with truffles*
pecho de ternera *breast of veal*
pechuga de pollo *breast of chicken*
pepinillos *gherkins*
pepino *cucumber*
peras *pears*
percebes *edible barnacle*
perdices a la campesina *partridges with vegetables*
perdices a la manchega *partridges in red wine, garlic, herbs, and pepper*
perdices escabechadas *marinated partridges*
perejil *parsley*
perritos calientes *hot dogs*
pescaditos fritos *fried fish*
pestiños *sugared pastries flavoured with aniseed*
pez espada *swordfish*
picadillo de ternera *minced veal*
pimienta *black pepper*
pimientos *peppers*
pimientos a la riojana *baked red peppers fried in oil and garlic*
pimientos morrones *a type of bell pepper*
pimientos verdes *green peppers*
piña al gratín *pineapple au gratin*
piña fresca *fresh pineapple*
pinchitos/pinchos *kebabs, snacks served in bars*
pinchos morunos *pork kebabs*
piñones *pine nuts*
pisto *ratatouille*
pisto manchego *vegetable marrow with onion and tomato*
plátanos *bananas*
plátanos flameados *flambéed bananas*
pollo *chicken*
pollo a la riojana *chicken with peppers and chillies*
pollo al ajillo *fried chicken with garlic*
pollo asado *roast chicken*
pollo braseado *braised chicken*
pollo en cacerola *chicken casserole*

pollo en pepitoria *chicken in wine with saffron, garlic, and almonds*

pollos tomateros con zanahorias *young chicken with carrots*

pomelo *grapefruit*

potaje castellano *thick broth*

potaje de ... ... *stew*

puchero canario *casserole of meat, chickpeas, and corn*

pulpitos con cebolla *baby octopus with onions*

pulpo *octopus*

puré de patatas *mashed potatoes, potato purée*

purrusalda *cod with leeks and potatoes*

Q

queso con membrillo *cheese with quince jelly*

queso de bola *Dutch cheese*

queso de Burgos *soft white cheese*

queso del país *local cheese*

queso de oveja *sheep's cheese*

queso gallego *a creamy cheese*

queso manchego *a hard, strong cheese*

quisquillas *shrimps*

R

rábanos *radishes*

ragout de ternera *veal ragoût*

rape a la americana *monkfish with brandy and herbs*

rape a la cazuela *stewed monkfish*

raya *skate*

rebozado *in batter*

redondo al horno *roast fillet of beef*

rellenos *stuffed*

remolacha *beetroot*

repollo *cabbage*

repostería de la casa *cakes baked on the premises*

requesón *cream cheese, cottage cheese*

revuelto de ... *scrambled eggs with ...*

revuelto de ajos tiernos *scrambled eggs with spring garlic*

revuelto de trigueros *scrambled eggs with asparagus*

revuelto mixto *scrambled eggs with mixed vegetables*

riñones *kidneys*

rodaballo *turbot (fish)*

romero *rosemary*

ron *rum*

roscas *sweet pastries*

S

sal *salt*

salchichas *sausages*

salchichas de Frankfurt *hot dog sausages*

salchichón *sausage similar to salami*

salmón ahumado *smoked salmon*

salmonetes *red mullet*

salmonetes en papillote *red mullet cooked in foil*

salmón frío *cold salmon*

salmorejo *sauce of bread, tomatoes, oil, vinegar, green pepper, and garlic*

salpicón de mariscos *shellfish in vinaigrette*

salsa *sauce*

salsa bechamel *white sauce*

salsa holandesa *hollandaise sauce*

sandía *watermelon*

sardinas a la brasa *barbecued sardines*

seco *dry*

semidulce *medium-sweet*

sesos *brains*

sesos a la romana *fried brains in batter*

sesos rebozados *brains in batter*

setas *mushrooms*

sidra *cider*

sobreasada *sausage with cayenne pepper*

solomillo *fillet steak*

solomillo con patatas *fillet steak with chips*

solomillo de ternera *fillet of veal*

solomillo de vaca *fillet of beef*

solomillo frío *cold roast beef*

sopa *soup*

sopa castellana *vegetable soup*

sopa de almendras *almond soup*

sopa de cola de buey *oxtail soup*

sopa de gallina *chicken soup*

sopa del día *soup of the day*

sopa de legumbres *vegetable soup*

sopa de marisco *fish and shellfish soup*

sopa de rabo de buey *oxtail soup*

sopa mallorquina *soup of tomato, meat, and eggs*

sopa sevillana *fish and mayonnaise soup*

soufflé de fresones *strawberry soufflé*

T

tallarines *noodles*

tallarines a la italiana *tagliatelle*

tarta *cake*

tarta de la casa *cake baked on the premises*

tarta de manzana *apple tart*

tencas *tench*

ternera asada *roast veal*

tocinillos del cielo *a very sweet crème caramel*

tomates *tomatoes*

tomillo *thyme*

torrijas *sweet pastries*

tortilla a la paisana *vegetable omelette*

tortilla a su gusto *omelette made to the customer's wishes*

tortilla de escabeche *fish omelette*

tortilla española *Spanish omelette with potato, onion, and garlic*

tortilla sacromonte *vegetable, brains, and sausage omelette*

tortillas variadas *assorted omelettes*

tournedó *fillet steak*

trucha *trout*

trucha ahumada *smoked trout*

trucha escabechada *marinated trout*

truchas a la marinera *trout in wine sauce*

truchas molinera *trout meunière (floured trout fried in butter)*

trufas *truffles*

turrón *nougat*

U, V

uvas *grapes*

verduras *vegetables*

vieiras *scallops*

vino de mesa/blanco /rosado/tinto *table/ white/rosé/red wine*

Z

zanahorias a la crema *creamed carrots*

zarzuela de mariscos *seafood stew*

zarzuela de pescados y mariscos *fish and shellfish stew*

zumo de ... ... *juice*

Dictionary
English to Spanish

The gender of a Spanish noun is indicated by the word for *the*: **el** and **la** (masculine and feminine singular) or their plural forms **los** (masculine) and **las** (feminine). Spanish adjectives (adj) vary according to the gender and number of the word they describe, and the masculine form is shown here. In general, adjectives that end in **-o** adopt an **-a** ending in the feminine form, and those that end in **-e** usually stay the same. For the plural form, an **-s** is added.

A

a un/una
able: to be able poder
about: about sixteen alrededor de dieciséis
accelerator el acelerador
accident el accidente
accommodation el alojamiento
accountant el/la contable
ache el dolor
adaptor el adaptador
address la dirección
adhesive el pegamento
admission charge el precio de entrada
after ... después de ...
aftershave el after-shave
again otra vez
against contra
agenda el orden del día
agency la agencia
AIDS el Sida
air el aire
air conditioning el aire acondicionado
aircraft el avión
airline la compañía aérea
air mail por avión
air mattress la colchoneta
airport el aeropuerto
airport bus el autobús del aeropuerto
aisle el pasillo
alarm clock el despertador
alcohol el alcohol
Algeria Argelia
all todo; *all the streets* todas las calles; *that's all* eso es todo
allergic alérgico
almost casi
alone solo
already ya
always siempre
am: I am soy/estoy

ambulance la ambulancia
America América
American el americano/la americana
and y; (after 'i' or 'h') e
angle-poise lamp el flexo
ankle el tobillo
another otro
answering machine el contestador automático
antifreeze el anticongelante
antique shop el anticuario
antiseptic el antiséptico
apartment el apartamento, el piso
aperitif el aperitivo
appetite el apetito
apple la manzana
application form el impreso de solicitud
appointment (business) la cita; (at hairdresser's) hora
apricot el albaricoque
April abril
are: you are (informal singular) eres/estás; (formal singular) es/está; (informal plural) sois/estáis; (formal plural) son/están; *we are* somos/estamos; *they are* son/están
arm el brazo
arrive llegar
art el arte
art gallery la galería de arte
artichoke la alcachofa
artist el/la artista
as: as soon as possible lo antes posible
ashtray el cenicero
asleep: he's asleep está dormido
aspirin la aspirina

asthmatic asmático
at: at the post office en Correos; *at night* por la noche; *at 3 o'clock* a las tres
Atlantic Ocean el Océano Atlántico
ATM el cajero automático
attic el ático
attractive (person) guapo; (object) bonito; (offer) atractivo
aubergines las berenjenas
August agosto
aunt la tía
Australia Australia
Australian el australiano/la australiana; (adj) australiano
automatic automático
available disponible
away: is it far away? ¿está lejos?; *go away!* ¡váyase!
awful horrible
axe el hacha
axle el eje

B

baby el niño pequeño, el bebé
baby wipes las toallitas para bebé
back (not front) la parte de atrás; (body) la espalda
backpack la mochila
bacon el bacon; *bacon and eggs* los huevos fritos con bacon
bad malo
bag la bolsa
bait el cebo
bake cocer al horno
bakery la panadería
balcony el balcón
Balearic Islands las (Islas) Baleares

ball (football) el balon;
(tennis etc) la pelota
ballpoint pen
el bolígrafo
banana el plátano
band (musicians)
la banda
bandage la venda
bank el banco
bank card la tarjeta
de banco
banknote el billete
de banco
bar (drinks) el bar
barbecue la barbacoa
barber la peluquería
de caballeros
bargain la ganga
basement el sótano
basin (sink) el lavabo
basket el cesto
basketball el baloncesto
bath el baño; *to have
a bath* darse un baño
bathing suit el bañador,
el traje de baño
bathroom el cuarto
de baño
battery (car) la batería;
(torch etc) la pila
Bay of Biscay el Golfo
de Vizcaya
be ser/estar
beach la playa
beach ball el balón
de playa
beans las judías
beard la barba
beautiful (object)
precioso; (person)
guapo
beauty products los
productos de belleza
because porque
bed la cama
bed linen la ropa de cama
bedroom el dormitorio
bedside lamp
la lamparilla de noche
bedside table la mesilla
de noche
bedspread la colcha
beef la carne de vaca
beer la cerveza
before ... antes de ...
beginner
el/la principiante
behind ... detrás de ...
beige beige
bell (church) la
campana; (door) el
timbre
below debajo de
belt el cinturón
beside al lado de
best (el) mejor
better mejor
between entre
bicycle la bicicleta
big grande
bill la cuenta

bin el contenedor de
basura
bin liner la bolsa de
basura
bird el pájaro
birthday el
cumpleaños; *happy
birthday!* ¡felicidades!
birthday present el
regalo de cumpleaños
biscuit la galleta
bite (by dog) la
mordedura; (by
insect) la picadura;
(verb: by dog)
morder; (by insect)
picar
black negro
blackberries las moras
blackcurrants las
grosellas negras
blanket la manta
bleach la lejía; (verb:
hair) teñir
blind (cannot see)
ciego
blinds las persianas
blister la ampolla
blizzard la ventisca
blond(e) (adj) rubio
blood la sangre
blood test el análisis
de sangre
blouse la blusa
blue azul
boarding pass la tarjeta
de embarque
boat el barco; (small)
la barca
body el cuerpo
boil (verb: water)
hervir; (egg etc) cocer
boiled hervido
bolt (on door) el
cerrojo; (verb) echar
el cerrojo
bone el hueso
bonnet (car) el capó
book el libro;(verb)
reservar
bookshop la librería
boot (footwear) la
bota; (car) el maletero
border el borde;
(between countries)
la frontera
boring aburrido
born: I was born in ...
nací en ...
both: both of them los
dos; *both of us* los
dos; *both ... and ...*
tanto ... como ...
bottle la botella
bottle opener
el abrebotellas
bottom el fondo; (part
of body) el trasero
bowl el cuenco
box la caja
box office la taquilla

boy el chico
boyfriend el novio
bra el sostén
bracelet la pulsera
braces (clothing) los
tirantes
brake el freno; (verb)
frenar
branch (of company)
la oficina
brandy el coñac
bread el pan
breakdown (car) la
avería; (nervous) la
crisis nerviosa; *I've
had a breakdown*
(car) he tenido una
avería
breakfast el desayuno
breathe respirar
bridge el puente;
(game) el bridge
briefcase la cartera
British británico
brochure el folleto
broken roto
brooch el broche
brother el hermano
brown marrón; (hair)
castaño; (skin)
moreno
bruise el cardenal
brush (paint) la
brocha; (cleaning)
el cepillo; (hair)
el cepillo del pelo;
(verb: hair) cepillar
el pelo
budget el presupuesto
bucket el cubo
builder el albañil
building el edificio
bull el toro
bullfight la corrida
de toros
bullfighter el torero
bullring la plaza de toros
bumper el parachoques
burglar el ladrón
burn la quemadura;
(verb) quemar
bus el autobús
business el negocio; *it's
none of your business*
no es asunto suyo
business card la tarjeta
de vista
bus station la estación
de autobuses
busy (bar) concurrido;
(engaged) ocupado
but pero
butcher's la carnicería
butter la mantequilla
button el botón
buy comprar
by: by the window junto
a la ventana; *by
Friday* para el viernes;
by myself yo solo;
written by escrito por

C

cabbage la col
cable car el teleférico
cable TV la television
    por cable
café el café
cage la jaula
cake (small) el pastel;
    (large) la tarta;
    sponge cake el
    bizcocho
cake shop la pastelería
calculator la calculadora
call: what's it called?
    ¿cómo se llama?
camcorder la
    videocámara
camera la máquina de
    fotos, la cámara de
    fotos
camper van la
    autocaravana
campfire la hoguera
camping gas el
    camping-gas
campsite el camping
camshaft el árbol de
    levas
can (tin) la lata; (verb:
    to be able) poder;
    can you ...?
    ¿puede ...?; I can't ...
    no puedo ...
Canada Canadá
Canadian canadiense
canal el canal
Canaries las (Islas)
    Canarias
candle la vela
can opener el abrelatas
cap (bottle) el tapón;
    (hat) la gorra
car el coche
caravan la roulotte
carburetor
    el carburador
card la tarjeta
cardigan la rebeca
careful prudente; be
    careful! ¡cuidado!
caretaker el portero,
    el encargado
car park
    el aparcamiento
carpenter el carpintero
carpet la alfombra
carriage (train) el vagón
carrot la zanahoria
car seat (for baby/child)
    el asiento infantil
case (suitcase) la
    maleta
cash el dinero; cobrar
    (verb); to pay cash
    pagar al contado
cashier el cajero
cashpoint el cajero
    automático
cassette la cassette,
    la cinta

cassette player
    el cassette
castanets las castañuelas
Castile Castilla
Castilian castellano
castle el castillo
cat el gato
Catalonia Cataluña
catch (bus etc) coger
cathedral la catedral
Catholic (adj) católico
cauliflower la coliflor
cave la cueva
ceiling el techo
cellar la bodega
cemetery el cementerio
central heating
    la calefacción central
centre el centro
certificate el certificado
chair la silla
change (money) el
    cambio; (verb:
    money) cambiar;
    (clothes) cambiarse;
    (trains etc) hacer
    transbordo
charger el cargador
check-in (desk)
    la (el mostrador de)
    facturación
check in (verb) facturar
check-out
    (supermarket)
    la caja
cheers! (toast) ¡salud!
cheese el queso
chemist la farmacia
cheque el cheque
chequebook el talonario
    de cheques
cherry la cereza
chess el ajedrez
chest (part of body)
    el pecho; (furniture)
    el arcón
chest of drawers
    la cómoda
chewing gum el chicle
chicken el pollo
child el niño/la niña
children los niños
children's ward la sala
    de pediatría
chimney la chimenea
china la porcelana
chips las patatas fritas
chocolate el chocolate;
    box of chocolates la
    caja de bombones;
    chocolate bar la
    tableta de chocolate
chop (food) la chuleta;
    (verb: cut) cortar
Christmas la navidad
church la iglesia
cigar el puro
cigarette el cigarrillo
cinema el cine
city la ciudad
city centre el centro

class la clase
classical music
    la música clásica
clean (adj) limpio
cleaner la asistenta
clear (obvious)
    evidente; (water)
    claro
clever listo
client el cliente
clock el reloj
close (near) cerca;
    (stuffy) sofocante;
    (verb) cerrar
closed cerrado
clothes la ropa
clubs (cards) tréboles
coat el abrigo
coat hanger la percha
cockroach la cucaracha
cocktail party el coctel
coffee el café
coin la moneda
cold (illness) el
    resfriado; (adj) frío;
    I have a cold tengo
    un resfriado; I'm
    cold tengo frío
collar el cuello; (of
    animal) el collar
collection (stamps etc)
    la colección; (postal)
    la recogida
colour el color
colour film la película
    en color
comb el peine; (verb)
    peinar
come venir; I come from
    ... soy de ...; we came
    last week llegamos la
    semana pasada; come
    here! ¡venga aquí!
come back volver
compact disc el disco
    compacto
compartment
    el compartimento
complicated complicado
computer el ordenador
computer games los
    vídeo-juegos
concert el concierto
conditioner (hair)
    el acondicionador
condom el condón
conductor (bus) el
    cobrador; (orchestra)
    el director
conference
    la conferencia
conference room la sala
    de conferencias
congratulations!
    ¡enhorabuena!
consulate el consulado
contact lenses las lentes
    de contacto
contraceptive
    el anticonceptivo
contract el contrato

cook el cocinero/
la cocinera; (verb)
guisar
cooker la cocina
cooking utensils los
utensilios de cocina
cool fresco
cork el corcho
corkscrew
el sacacorchos
corner (of street) la
esquina; (of room)
el rincón
corridor el pasillo
cosmetics los cosméticos
cost (verb) costar;
what does it cost?
¿cuánto cuesta?
cot la cuna
cotton el algodón
cotton wool el algodón
cough la tos; (verb)
toser
cough drops las pastillas
para la garganta
country (state) el país
countryside el campo
cousin el primo/la prima
crab el cangrejo
cramp el calambre
crayfish las cigalas
cream (dairy) la nata;
(lotion) la crema
credit card la tarjeta de
crédito
crib el capazo
crisps las patatas fritas
crowded lleno
cruise el crucero
crutches las muletas
cry (weep) llorar;
(shout) gritar
cucumber el pepino
cuff links los gemelos
cup la taza
cupboard el armario
curlers los rulos
curls los rizos
curry el curry
curtain la cortina
cushion el cojín
customs la aduana
cut la cortadura; (verb)
cortar
cycling el ciclismo

D

dad papá
dairy products los
productos lácteos
damp húmedo
dance el baile; (verb)
bailar
dangerous peligroso
dark oscuro; *dark blue*
azul oscuro
daughter la hija
day el día
dead muerto
deaf sordo

dear (person) querido
December diciembre
deck of cards la baraja
decorator el pintor
deep profundo
delayed retrasado
deliberately
a propósito
delicatessen
la charcutería
delivery la entrega
dentist el/la dentista
dentures la dentadura
postiza
deny negar
deodorant
el desodorante
department
el departamento
department store los
grandes almacenes
departure la salida
departures las salidas
deposit la señal
designer el diseñador/
la diseñadora
desk la mesa de
escritorio
dessert el postre
develop (film) revelar
diabetic diabético
diamonds (jewels) los
diamantes; (cards)
los diamantes
diarrhoea la diarrea
diary la agenda
dictionary el diccionario
die morir
diesel (oil) fuel-oil;
(adj: engine) diesel
different diferente;
that's different! ¡eso
es distinto!; *I'd like
a different one*
quisiera otro distinto
difficult difícil
dining room el comedor
dinner la cena
dinner party la cena
dirty sucio
disabled minusválido
discount el descuento
dish cloth el paño de
cocina
dishwasher el
lavavajillas
disposable nappies los
pañales desechables
divorced divorciado
do hacer
dock el muelle
doctor el médico/
la médica
document el documento
dog el perro
doll la muñeca
dollar el dólar
door la puerta
double room
la habitación doble
doughnut el dónut

down hacia abajo
drawing pin
la chincheta
dress el vestido
drink la bebida; (verb)
beber; *would you like
something to drink?*
¿quiere beber algo?
drinking water agua
potable
drive (verb) conducir
driver el conductor
driving licence el carnet
de conducir
drops las gotas
drunk borracho
dry seco; (sherry) fino
dry cleaner la tintorería
during durante
dustbin el cubo de la
basura
duster el trapo del polvo
duty-free libre de
impuestos; *duty-free
shop* el duty-free
duvet el edredón

E

each (every) cada;
20 euros each veinte
euros cada uno
ear (inner) el oído;
(outer) la oreja;
ears las orejas
early temprano
earrings los pendientes
east este; *the East* el
Este
easy fácil
eat comer
egg el huevo
eight ocho
eighteen dieciocho
eighty ochenta
either: either of them
cualquiera de ellos;
either ... or ...
o bien ... o ...
elastic elástico
elbow el codo
electric eléctrico
electrician
el/la electricista
electricity la electricidad
eleven once
else: something else
algo más; *someone
else* alguien más;
somewhere else en
otro sitio
email el email, el correo
electrónico
email address la
dirección de email
embarrassing
embarazoso
embassy la embajada
embroidery el bordado
emergency la emergencia
emergency brake

(train) el freno de emergencia

emergency department el servicio de urgencias

emergency exit la salida de emergencia

employee el empleado

empty vacío

end el final

engaged (marriage) prometido/prometida; (telephone) ocupado

engine (motor) el motor

engineering la ingeniería

England Inglaterra

English inglés

Englishman el inglés

Englishwoman la inglesa

enlargement la ampliación

enough bastante

entertainment las diversiones

entrance la entrada

envelope el sobre

epileptic epiléptico

eraser la goma de borrar

escalator la escalera mecánica

especially sobre todo

espresso el café solo

estimate el presupuesto

evening la tarde

every cada; every day todos los días

everyone todos

everything todo

everywhere por todas partes

example el ejemplo; for example por ejemplo

excellent excelente

excess baggage exceso de equipaje

exchange (verb) cambiar

exchange rate el cambio

excursion la excursión

excuse me! (to get attention) ¡oiga, por favor!; (when sneezing etc) ¡perdón!; excuse me, please (to get past) ¿me hace el favor?

executive el ejecutivo

exhaust el tubo de escape

exhibition la exposición

exit la salida

expensive caro

extension cord el cable alargador

eye el ojo

eyebrow la ceja

F

face la cara

faint (unclear) tenue; (verb) desmayarse; I feel faint estoy mareado

fair (unclear) la feria; it's not fair no hay derecho

false teeth la dentadura postiza

family la familia

fan (enthusiast) el fan; (football) el hincha; (ventilator) el ventilador; (handheld) el abanico

fantastic fantástico

far lejos; how far is it to ...? ¿qué distancia hay a ...?

fare el billete, la tarifa

farm la granja

farmer el granjero

fashion la moda

fast rápido

fat (adj) gordo; (on meat) la grasa

father el padre

fax el fax; (verb) enviar por fax

February febrero

feel (touch) tocar; I feel hot tengo calor; I feel like ... me apetece ...; I don't feel well no me encuentro bien

felt-tip pen el rotulador

fence la cerca

ferry el ferry

fiancé el prometido

fiancée la prometida

field (of grass etc) el campo; (of study) la especialidad

fifteen quince

fifty cincuenta

fig el higo

figures los números

filling (in tooth) el empaste; (in sandwich, cake) el relleno

film la película

filter el filtro

filter papers los papeles de filtro

finger el dedo

fire el fuego; (blaze) el incendio

fire extinguisher el extintor

fireplace la chimenea

fireworks los fuegos artificiales

first primero; first aid primeros auxilios

first class de primera

first floor el primer piso

first name el nombre de pila

fish el pez; (food) el pescado

fishing la pesca; to go fishing ir a pescar

fishmonger's la pescadería

five cinco

fizzy water el agua con gas

flag la bandera

flash (camera) el flash

flat (level) plano

flat tyre la rueda pinchada

flavour el sabor

flea la pulga

flea spray el spray antipulgas

flight el vuelo

floor el suelo; (storey) el piso

flour la harina

flower la flor

flowerbed el parterre

flute la flauta

fly (insect) la mosca; (verb: of plane, insect) volar; (of person) viajar en avión

flyover el paso elevado

fog la niebla

folk music la música folklórica

food la comida

food poisoning la intoxicación alimenticia

foot el pie

football el fútbol; (ball) el balón

for: for me para mí; what for? ¿para qué?; for a week (para) una semana

foreigner el extranjero/la extranjera

forest el bosque; (tropical) la selva

forget olvidar

fork el tenedor; (garden) la horca

forty cuarenta

fountain la fuente

fountain pen la (pluma) estilográfica

four cuatro

fourteen catorce

fourth cuarto

France Francia

free (not engaged) libre; (no charge) gratis

freezer el congelador

French francés

Friday viernes

fridge el frigorífico

fried frito

friend el amigo/la amiga

friendly simpático

fringe (hair) el flequillo

front: in front of ... delante de ...

frost la escarcha

frozen foods los congelados

fruit la fruta

fruit juice el zumo de frutas

fry freír

frying pan la sartén

full lleno; *I'm full (up)* estoy lleno

full board pensión completa

funny divertido; (odd) raro

furniture los muebles

G

garage (for parking) el garage; (for repairs) el taller

garden el jardín

garden centre el vivero

garlic el ajo

gas-permeable lenses las lentes de contacto semi-rígidas

gate la puerta, la verja; (at airport) la puerta de embarque

gay (homosexual) gay

gearbox la caja de cambios

gear stick la palanca de velocidades

gel (hair) el gel

German alemán

Germany Alemania

get (fetch) traer; *have you got ...?* ¿tiene ...?; *to get the train* coger el tren

get back: we get back tomorrow nos volvemos mañana; *to get something back* recobrar algo

get in (of train etc) subirse; (of person) llegar

get off (bus etc) bajarse

get on (bus etc) subirse

get out bajarse; (bring out) sacar

get up (rise) levantarse

Gibraltar Gibraltar

gift el regalo

gin la ginebra

ginger (spice) el jengibre

girl la chica

girlfriend la novia

give dar

glad alegre

glass (material) el cristal; (for drinking) el vaso, la copa

glasses las gafas

gloss prints las copias con brillo

gloves los guantes

glue el pegamento

go ir

gold el oro

good bueno; *good!* ¡bien!

good afternoon buenas tardes

goodbye adiós

good evening buenas noches

good morning buenos días

government el gobierno

granddaughter la nieta

grandfather el abuelo

grandmother la abuela

grandparents los abuelos

grandson el nieto

grapes las uvas

grass la hierba

Great Britain Gran Bretaña

green verde

greengrocer's la verdulería

grey gris

grill la parrilla

grilled a la plancha

grocer's el ultramarinos, la tienda de comestibles

ground floor la planta baja

groundsheet la lona impermeable, el suelo aislante

guarantee la garantía; (verb) garantizar

guest la invitada

guide el/la guía

guide book la guía turística

guided tour la visita con guía

guitar la guitarra

gun (rifle) la escopeta; (pistol) la pistola

H

hair el pelo

haircut el corte de pelo

hairdresser's la peluquería

hairdryer el secador (de pelo)

hairspray la laca

half medio; *half an hour* media hora

half board media pensión

ham el jamón

hamburger la hamburguesa

hammer el martillo

hamster el hámster

hand la mano

handbag el bolso

handbrake el freno de mano

handle (door) el picaporte

hand luggage el equipaje de mano

handshake el apretón de manos

handsome guapo

hangover la resaca

happy contento, feliz

harbour el puerto

hard duro; (difficult) difícil

hardware store la ferretería

hat el sombrero; (woollen) el gorro

have tener; *I don't have ... no tengo ...; do you have ...?* ¿tiene ...?; *I have to go* tengo que irme ; *can I have ...?* ¿me pone ...?

hay fever la fiebre del heno

he él

head la cabeza

headache el dolor de cabeza

headlights los faros

headphones los auriculares

hear oír

hearing aid el audífono

heart el corazón

hearts (cards) los corazones

heater la estufa

heating la calefacción

heavy pesado

hedge el seto

heel el talón; (shoe) el tacón

hello hola; (on phone) dígame

help la ayuda; (verb) ayudar

hepatitis la hepatitis

her: it's for her es para ella; *her book* su libro; *her shoes* sus zapatos; *it's hers* es suyo; *give it to her* déselo

high alto

highway code el código de la circulación

hiking el senderismo

hill el monte

him: it's for him es para él; *give it to him* déselo

hire (verb) alquilar

his: his book su libro; *his shoes* sus zapatos; *it's his* es suyo

history la historia

hitchhike hacer auto-stop

HIV positive seropositivo

hobby el hobby

holiday las vacaciones

home la casa; *at home* en casa
homeopathy la homeopatía
honest honrado; (sincere) sincero
honey la miel
honeymoon el viaje de novios
horn (car) el claxon; (animal) el cuerno
horrible horrible
hospital el hospital
hostess la anfitriona
hour la hora
house la casa
household products los productos del hogar
hovercraft el aerodeslizador
how? ¿cómo?
how are you? ¿qué tal?
hundred cien
hungry: I'm hungry tengo hambre
hurry: I'm in a hurry tengo prisa
husband el marido
hydrofoil la hidroaleta

I

I yo
ice el hielo
ice cream el helado
ice skates los patines para hielo
if si
ignition el encendido
immediately inmediatamente
impossible imposible
in en; *in English* en inglés; *in the hotel* en el hotel; *in Barcelona* en Barcelona; *he's not in* no está
included incluido
indicator el intermitente
indigestion indigestión
inexpensive barato
infection la infección
information la información
inhaler (for asthma etc) el spray, el inhalador
injection la inyección
injury la herida
ink la tinta
inn la fonda
inner tube la cámara (neumática)
insect el insecto
insect repellent la loción anti-mosquitos
insomnia el insomnio
instant coffee el café instantáneo
insurance el seguro

interesting interesante
internet el internet
interpret interpretar
interpreter el/la intérprete
invitation la invitación
invoice la factura
Ireland Irlanda
Irish irlandés/ irlandesa
iron (metal) el hierro; (for clothes) la plancha;(verb) planchar
is es/está
island la isla
it lo/la
Italian (adj) italiano/ italiana (m/f)
Italy Italia
its su

J

jacket la chaqueta
jam la mermelada
January enero
jazz el jazz
jeans los tejanos, los vaqueros
jellyfish la medusa
jeweller's la joyería
job el trabajo
jog (verb) hacer footing
joke la broma; (funny story) el chiste
journey el viaje
juice el zumo
July julio
June junio
just (only) sólo; *it's just arrived* acaba de llegar

K

kettle el hervidor de agua
key la llave
keyboard el teclado
kidney el riñón
kilo el kilo
kilometre el kilómetro
kitchen la cocina
knee la rodilla
knife el cuchillo
knit hacer punto
knitwear los artículos de punto
know saber; (person, place) conocer; *I don't know* no sé

L

label la etiqueta
lace el encaje
laces (shoe) los cordones (de los zapatos)
lady la señora
lake el lago
lamb el cordero
lamp la lámpara, el flexo
lampshade la pantalla

land la tierra; (verb) aterrizar
language el idioma
large grande
last (final) último; *at last!* ¡por fin! ; *last week* la semana pasada
late: it's getting late se está haciendo tarde; *the bus is late* el autobús se ha retrasado
later más tarde
laugh reír
laundrette la lavandería automática
laundry (dirty) la ropa sucia; (washed) la colada
law el derecho
lawn el césped
lawn mower la maquina cortacésped
lawyer el abogado/ la abogada
laxative el laxante
lazy perezoso
lead la correa
leaf la hoja
leaflet el folleto
learn aprender
leather el cuero
lecture theatre el anfiteatro
lecturer (university) el profesor/la profesora de universidad
left (not right) izquierdo; *there's nothing left* no queda nada
leg la pierna
lemon el limón
lemonade la limonada
length la longitud
lens la lente
less menos
lesson la clase
letter (mail) la carta; (of alphabet) la letra
lettuce la lechuga
library la biblioteca
licence el permiso
life la vida
lift el ascensor
light la luz; (weight) ligero; (not dark) claro
light bulb la bombilla
lighter el encendedor
lighter fuel el gas para el encendedor
light meter el fotómetro
like: I like ... me gusta ...; *I like swimming* me gusta nadar; *it's like ...* es como ...; *like this one* como éste
lime (fruit) la lima
line la cola; (phone etc) línea; (verb) hacer cola
lipstick la barra de labios

liqueur el licor
list la lista
literature la literatura
litre el litro
litter la basura
little (small) pequeño;
  it's a little big es un
  poco grande; *just a*
  little sólo un poquito
liver el hígado
living room el cuarto
  de estar
lobster la langosta
lollipop el chupa-chups
long largo
lost property office
  la oficina de objetos
  perdidos
lot: a lot mucho
loud alto
lounge (in house)
  el cuarto de estar;
  (in hotel etc) el salón
love el amor; (verb)
  querer; *I love Spain*
  me encanta España
lover el/la amante
low bajo
luck: good luck! ¡suerte!
luggage el equipaje
luggage rack la rejilla
  de equipajes
lunch la comida

M

mad loco
madam señora
magazine la revista
mail el correo
main course el plato
  principal
main road la calle
  principal
Majorca Mallorca
make hacer
make-up el maquillaje
man el hombre
manager el/la gerente,
  el jefe; (hotel) el
  director/la directora
many muchos/muchas;
  many thanks muchas
  gracias; *many people*
  mucha gente; *how*
  many ¿cuántos?; *too*
  many demasiados;
  not many no muchos
map el mapa; *town*
  map/plan el plano
marble el mármol
March marzo
margarine la margarina
market el mercado
marmalade la
  mermelada de naranja
married casado
mascara el rímel
mass (church) la misa
match (light) la cerilla;
  (sport) el partido

material (cloth) la tela
matter: it doesn't matter
  no importa
mattress el colchón
May mayo
maybe quizás
me: it's for me es para
  mí; *give it to me* démelo
meal la comida
mean: what does this
  mean? ¿qué significa
  esto?
meat la carne
mechanic el mecánico
medicine la medicina
Mediterranean
  el Mediterráneo
medium (sherry)
  amontillado
medium-dry (wine)
  semi-seco
meeting la reunión
melon el melón
menu la carta; *set menu*
  el menú (del día)
message el recado,
  el mensaje
metro station
  la estación de metro
microwave
  el microondas
midday el mediodía
middle: in the middle
  en el centro
midnight medianoche
milk la leche
mine: it's mine es mío
mineral water el agua
  mineral
minute el minuto
mirror el espejo
Miss Señorita
mistake la equivocación
mobile phone
  el teléfono móvil,
  el teléfono celular
modem el modem
Monday lunes
money el dinero
monitor el monitor
month el mes
monument
  el monumento
moon la luna
moped el ciclomotor
more más
morning la mañana;
  in the morning por la
  mañana
Morocco Marruecos
mosaic el mosaico
mosquito el mosquito
mother la madre
motorboat la motora
motorcycle
  la motocicleta
motorway la autopista
mountain la montaña
mountain bike
  la bicicleta de
  montaña

mouse el ratón
mousse (for hair) la
  espuma moldeadora
moustache el bigote
mouth la boca
move (verb:
  something) mover;
  (oneself) moverse;
  (house) mudarse de
  casa; *don't move!* ¡no
  se mueva!
movie la película
Mr Señor
Mrs Señora
much: much better
  mucho mejor; *much*
  slower mucho más
  despacio
mug la jarrita
Mum mama
museum el museo
mushrooms
  los champiñones,
  las setas
music la música
musical instrument
  el instrumento musical
musician el músico
music system el equipo
  de música
mussels los mejillones
must (to have to) tener
  que *I must ...* tengo
  que ...
mustard la mostaza
my: my book mi libro;
  my keys mis llaves

N

nail (metal) el clavo;
  (finger) la uña
nail clippers el cortauñas
nailfile la lima de uñas
nail polish el esmalte
  de uñas
name el nombre; *what's*
  your name? ¿cómo se
  llama usted?; *my*
  name is... me llamo...
napkin la servilleta
nappy el pañal
narrow estrecho
near: near the door
  junto a la puerta; *near*
  New York cerca de
  New York
necessary necesario
neck el cuello
necklace el collar
need (verb) necesitar;
  I need ... necesito ...;
  there's no need no
  hace falta
needle la aguja
negative (photo)
  el negativo
neither: neither of them
  ninguno de ellos;
  neither ... nor ...
  ni ... ni ...

nephew el sobrino

never nunca

new nuevo

news las noticias

newsagent's el kiosko de periódicos

newspaper el periódico

New Zealand Nueva Zelanda

New Zealander el neozelandés/ la neozelandesa

next próximo, siguiente; *next week* la semana que viene; *what next?* ¿y ahora qué?

nice bonito; (pleasant) agradable; (to eat) bueno

niece la sobrina

night la noche

nightclub la discoteca

nightgown el camisón

night porter el vigilante nocturno

nine nueve

nineteen diecinueve

ninety noventa

no (response) no; *I have no money* no tengo dinero

nobody nadie

noisy ruidoso

noon mediodía

north el norte

Northern Ireland Irlanda del Norte

nose la nariz

not no; *he's not ...* no es/está ...

notebook el cuaderno

notepad el bloc

nothing nada

novel la novela

November noviembre

now ahora

nowhere en ninguna parte

nudist el/la nudista

number el número

number plate la matrícula

nurse el enfermo/ la enferma

nut (fruit) la nuez; (for bolt) la tuerca

O

oars los remos

occasionally de vez en cuando

occupied ocupado

October octubre

octopus el pulpo

of de

office (place) la oficina; (room) el despacho

office block el bloque de oficinas

often a menudo

oil el aceite

ointment la pomada

OK vale

old viejo; *how old are you?* ¿cuántos años tiene?

olive la aceituna

olive oil el aceite de oliva

olive tree el olivo

omelette la tortilla

on ... en ...

one uno

onion la cebolla

only sólo

open (adj) abierto; (verb) abrir

opening times el horario de apertura

operating theatre el quirófano

operation la operación

operator la operadora

opposite: opposite the hotel enfrente del hotel

optician el/la oculista

or o

orange (fruit) la naranja; (colour) naranja

orchestra la orquesta

order el pedido

organ (music) el órgano

other: the other (one) el otro

our nuestro; *it's ours* es nuestro

out: he's out no está

outside fuera; *external* externa

oven el horno

over ... encima de ...; (more than) más de ...; *it's over the road* está al otro lado de la calle; *when the party is over* cuando termine la fiesta; *over there* allí

overtake (in car) adelantar

oyster la ostra

P

package el paquete

packet el paquete; (cigarettes) la cajetilla; (sweets, crisps) la bolsa

padlock el candado

page la página

pain el dolor

paint la pintura

pair el par

palace el palacio

pale pálido

pancakes las crepes

paper el papel; (newspaper) el periódico

paraffin la parafina

parcel el paquete

pardon? ¿cómo dice?

parents los padres

park el parque; (verb) aparcar; *no parking* prohibido aparcar

parsley el perejil

parting (hair) la raya

party (celebration) la fiesta; (group) el grupo; (political) el partido

passenger el pasajero

passport el pasaporte

password la contraseña

pasta la pasta

path el camino

pavement la acera

pay pagar

payment el pago

peach el melocotón

peanuts los cacahuetes

pear la pera

pearl la perla

peas los guisantes

pedestrian el peatón

pedestrian zone la zona peatonal

peg la pinza

pen la pluma

pencil el lápiz

pencil sharpener el sacapuntas

penknife la navaja

pen pal el amigo/ la amiga por correspondencia

people la gente

pepper la pimienta; (red, green) el pimiento

peppermints las pastillas de menta

per: per night por noche

perfect perfecto

perfume el perfume

perhaps quizás

perm la permanente

pet passport el pasaporte de animales

petrol la gasolina

petrol station la gasolinera

pets los animales de compañía; los animales domésticos

phone book la guía telefónica

phone booth la cabina telefónica

phonecard la tarjeta telefónica

photocopier la fotocopiadora

photograph la foto(grafía); (verb) fotografiar

photographer el fotógrafo

phrase book el libro de frases

piano el piano

pickpocket el carterista
picnic el picnic
piece el pedazo
pill la pastilla
pillow la almohada
pilot el piloto
PIN el pin
pin el alfiler
pine (tree) el pino
pineapple la piña
pink rosa
pipe (for smoking)
  la pipa; (for water)
  la tubería
piston el piston
pitch la plaza
pizza la pizza
place el lugar; *at your
  place* en su casa
plant la planta
plaster la tirita
plastic el plástico
plastic bag la bolsa de
  plástico
plastic wrap el plástico
  para envolver
plate el plato
platform (train) el
  andén
play (theatre) la obra
  de teatro; (verb) jugar
please por favor
pleased to meet you
  encantado/encantada
plug (electrical)
  el enchufe, (sink)
  el tapón
plumber el fontanero/
  la fontanera
pocket el bolsillo
poison el veneno
police la policía
police officer el policía
police report la denuncia
police station la comisaría
politics la política
poor pobre; (bad
  quality) malo
pop music la música pop
pork la carne de cerdo
port (harbour)
  el puerto; (drink)
  el oporto
porter (hotel)
  el conserje
Portugal Portugal
Portuguese portugués
possible posible
post el correo; (verb)
  echar al correo
postbox el buzón
postcard la postal
postcode el código postal
poster el póster
postman el cartero
post office (la oficina de)
  Correos
potato la patata
poultry las aves
pound (sterling)
  la libra

powder el polvo;
  (cosmetic) los polvos
pram el cochecito
prawns las gambas
prefer preferir
pregnant embarazada
prescription la receta
pretty bonito; (quite)
  bastante
price el precio
priest el cura
printer la impresora
private privado
problem el problema
profession la profesión
professor el catedrático
profits los beneficios
prohibited prohibido
protection factor (SPF)
  el factor de protección
public público
public holiday el día
  de fiesta
public swimming pool
  la piscina municipal
pull tirar de
puncture el pinchazo
purple morado
purse la cartera,
  el monedero
push empujar
pushchair la sillita de
  ruedas
put poner
pyjamas el pijama
Pyrenees los Pirineos

Q

quality la calidad
quarter el cuarto
question la pregunta
quick rápido
quiet tranquilo;
  (person) callado
quite (fairly) bastante;
  (fully) completamente

R

rabbit el conejo
radiator el radiador
radio la radio
radish el rábano
rake el rastrillo
railway el ferrocarril
rain la lluvia
raincoat la gabardina
rainforest la selva
raisins las pasas
raspberry la frambuesa
rare (uncommon)
  raro; (steak) poco
  hecho, poco pasado
rat la rata
razor blades
  las cuchillas de afeitar
read leer
ready listo
ready meals
  los platos preparados

receipt el recibo
reception la recepción
receptionist
  el/la recepcionista
record (music) el disco;
  (sport etc) el récord
record player
  el tocadiscos
record store la tienda
  de discos
red rojo; (wine) tinto
refreshments
  los refrescos
refrigerator el frigorífico
registered post correo
  certificado
relative el pariente
relax relajarse; (rest)
  descansar
religion la religión
remember: I remember
  me acuerdo; *I don't
  remember* no me
  acuerdo
repair arreglar
report el informe
reservation la reserva
rest (remainder) el
  resto; (verb: relax)
  descansar
restaurant
  el restaurante
restaurant car
  el vagón-restaurante
return (come back)
  volver, (give back)
  devolver
return ticket el billete
  de ida y vuelta
rice el arroz
rich rico
right (correct) correcto;
  (not left) derecho
ring (for finger) el anillo
ripe maduro
river el río
road la carretera
roasted asado
robbery el robo
rock (stone) la roca
roll (bread) el bollo
roof el tejado
room la habitación;
  (space) el sitio
room service el servicio
  de habitaciones
rope la cuerda
rose la rosa
round (circular)
  redondo
roundabout la rotonda
row (verb) remar
rowing boat la barca
  de remos
rubber (material)
  la goma
rubber band la goma
rubbish la basura
ruby (stone) el rubí
rug (mat) la alfombra;
  (blanket) la manta

rugby el rugby
ruins las ruinas
ruler (for measuring) la regla
rum el ron
run (verb) correr
runway la pista

S

sad triste
safe (not dangerous) seguro
safety pin el imperdible
sailboard la tabla de windsurfing
sailing la vela
salad la ensalada
sale (at reduced prices) las rebajas
sales las ventas
salmon el salmón
salt la sal
same: the same dress el mismo vestido; *the same people* la misma gente; *same again, please* lo mismo otra vez, por favor
sand la arena
sandals las sandalias
sand dunes las dunas
sandwich el bocadillo
sanitary towels las compresas
Saturday sábado
sauce la salsa
saucepan el cazo
saucer el platillo
sauna la sauna
sausage la salchicha
say decir; *what did you say?* ¿qué ha dicho?; *how do you say ...?* ¿cómo se dice ...?
scampi las gambas
scarf la bufanda; (head) el pañuelo
schedule el programa
school la escuela
science las ciencias
scissors las tijeras
Scotland Escocia
Scottish escocés/escocesa
screen la pantalla
screw el tornillo
screwdriver el destornillador
sea el mar
seafood los mariscos
seat el asiento
seat belt el cinturón de seguridad
second el segundo
second class de segunda
see ver; *I can't see* no veo; *I see* comprendo
self-employed (person) el autónomo/la autónoma

sell vender
seminar el seminario
send mandar
separate (adj) distinto
separated separado
September septiembre
serious serio
seven siete
seventeen diecisiete
seventy setenta
several varios
sew coser
shampoo el champú
shave el afeitado; *to have a shave* afeitarse
shaving foam la espuma de afeitar
shawl el chal
she ella
sheet la sábana; (of paper) la hoja
shell la concha
shellfish mariscos
sherry el jerez
ship el barco
shirt la camisa
shoelaces los cordones de los zapatos
shoe polish la crema de zapatos
shoes los zapatos
shoe shop la zapatería
shop la tienda
shopping la compra; *to go shopping* ir de compras
short corto; (height) bajo
shorts los pantalones cortos
shoulder el hombro
shower (bath) la ducha; (rain) el chaparrón
shower gel el gel de ducha
shrimp las quisquillas
shutter (camera) el obturador; (window) el postigo
sick: I feel sick tengo náuseas; *to be sick* (vomit) devolver
side (edge) el borde
side lights las luces de posición
sights: the sights of ... los lugares de interés de ...
sightseeing el turismo
silk la seda
silver (metal) la plata; (colour) plateado
simple sencillo
sing cantar
single (ticket) de ida; (only) único; (unmarried) soltero/soltera
single room la habitación individual
sink el fregadero

sister la hermana
six seis
sixteen dieciséis
sixty sesenta
skid patinar
skiing: to go skiing ir a esquiar
skin cleanser la leche limpiadora
ski resort la estación de esquí
skirt la falda
skis los esquís
sky el cielo
sleep el sueño; (verb) dormir
sleeper car el coche-cama
sleeping bag el saco de dormir
sleeping pill el somnífero
sleeve la manga
slip (underwear) la combinacíon
slippers las zapatillas
slow lento
small pequeño
smell el olor; (verb) oler
smile la sonrisa; (verb) sonreír
smoke el humo; (verb) fumar
snack la comida ligera
snow la nieve
so: so good tan bueno; *not so much* no tanto
soaking solution (for contact lenses) la solución limpiadora
soap el jabón
socks los calcetines
soda water la soda
sofa el sofa
soft blando
soil la tierra
somebody alguien
somehow de algún modo
something algo
sometimes a veces
somewhere en alguna parte
son el hijo
song la canción
sorry! ¡perdón!; I'm sorry perdón/lo siento; *sorry?* (pardon) ¿cómo dice?
soup la sopa
south el sur
South America Sudamérica
souvenir el recuerdo
spade la pala
spades (cards) las picas
Spain España
Spaniard el español/la española
speak hablar; *do you speak ...?* ¿habla ...?; *I don't speak ...* no hablo ...

speed la velocidad
speed limit el límite de velocidad
spider la araña
spinach las espinacas
spoon la cuchara
sport el deporte
sports centre el centro deportivo
spring (mechanical) el muelle; (season) la primavera
square (in town) la plaza; (adj) cuadrado
staircase la escalera
stairs las escaleras
stamp el sello
stapler la grapadora
star la estrella
start (beginning) el principio; (verb) empezar
starters los entrantes
statement la declaración
station la estación
statue la estatua
steak el filete
steal robar; *it's been stolen* lo han robado
steamed al vapor
steamer (boat) el vapor
stepdaughter la hijastra
stepfather el padastro
stepmother la madastra
stepson el hijastro
still water el agua sin gas
stockings las medias
stomach el estómago
stomach-ache el dolor de estómago
stop (bus) la parada; (verb) parar; *stop!* ¡alto!
storm la tormenta
strawberries las fresas
stream (small river) el arroyo
street la calle
string la cuerda
stroller la sillita de ruedas
strong fuerte
student el/la estudiante
stupid estúpido
suburbs las afueras
sugar el azúcar
suit (clothing) el traje; *it suits you* te sienta bien
suitcase la maleta
sun el sol
sunbathe tomar el sol
sunburn la quemadura de sol
Sunday domingo
sunglasses las gafas de sol
sunshade la sombrilla
sunstroke la insolación

suntan: to get a suntan broncearse
suntan lotion la loción bronceadora
suntanned bronceado
supermarket el supermercado
supper la cena
supplement el suplemento
suppository el supositorio
sure seguro
surname el apellido
sweat el sudor; (verb) sudar
sweater el jersey
sweatshirt la sudadera
sweet (adj: not sour) dulce; *sweets* los caramelos (m)
swim (verb) nadar
swimming la natación
swimming pool la piscina
swimming trunks el bañador
switch el interruptor
synagogue la sinagoga
syringe la jeringuilla
syrup el jarabe

T

table la mesa
tablet la pastilla
take tomar
take off el despegue
talcum powder los polvos de talco
talk la charla; (verb) hablar
tall alto
tampons los tampones
tangerine la mandarina
tap el grifo
tapestry el tapiz
taxi el taxi
taxi rank la parada de taxis
tea el té
teacher el profesor/ la profesora
technician el técnico
telephone el teléfono; (verb) llamar por teléfono
television la televisión
temperature la temperatura; (fever) la fiebre
ten diez
tennis el tenis
tent la tienda (de campaña)
tent peg la estaquilla, la estaca
tent pole el mástil
terminal la terminal
terrace la terraza
test la prueba

than que
thank (verb) agradecer; *thank you* gracias; *thanks* gracias
that ese/esa, eso; *that bus* ese autobús; *that man* ese hombre; *that woman* esa mujer; *what's that?* ¿qué es eso?; *I think that ...* creo que ...; *that one* ése/ésa
the el/la; (plural) los/las
theatre el teatro
their: their room su habitación; *their books* sus libros; *it's theirs* es suyo
them: it's for them es para ellos/ellas; *give it to them* déselo
then entonces; (after) después
there allí; there is/are ... hay ...; *is/are there ...?* ¿hay ?
these: these men estos hombres; *these women* estas mujeres; *these are mine* éstos son míos
they ellos/ellas
thick grueso
thief el ladrón
thin delgado
think pensar; *I think so* creo que sí; *I'll think about it* lo pensaré
third tercero
thirsty: I'm thirsty tengo sed
thirteen trece
thirty treinta
this: this one éste/ésta; *this man* este hombre; *this woman* esta mujer; *what's this?* ¿qué es esto?; *this is Mr ...* éste es el señor ...
those: those men esos hombres; *those women* esas mujeres
thousand mil
throat la garganta
through por
three tres
thunderstorm la tormenta
Thursday jueves
ticket (train etc) el billete; (theatre etc) la entrada
ticket office la taquilla
tide la marea
tie la corbata; (verb) atar
tight ajustado
tights las medias, los pantis
time tiempo; *what's the time?* ¿qué hora es?
timetable el horario

tin la hojalata
tip (end) la punta; (money) la propina
tired cansado
tissues los pañuelos de papel
to: to America a América; *to the station* a la estación; *to the doctor* al médico
toast la tostada
tobacco el tabaco
tobacconist el estanco
today hoy
together juntos
toilet (room in house) el baño; (bathroom item) el váter; (in public establishment) los servicos
toilet paper el papel higiénico
toilets (men) los servicios de caballeros; (women) los servicios de señoras
tomato el tomate
tomato juice el zumo de tomate
tomorrow mañana
tongue la lengua
tonic la tónica
tonight esta noche
too (also) también; (excessively) demasiado
tooth el diente; *back tooth* la muela
toothache el dolor de muelas
toothbrush el cepillo de dientes
toothpaste la pasta dentífrica
torch la linterna
tour la excursión
tourist el/la turista
tourist office la oficina de turismo
towel la toalla
tower la torre
town el pueblo
town hall el ayuntamiento
toy el juguete
trade fair la feria
track suit el chandal
tractor el tractor
tradition la tradición
traffic el tráfico
traffic jam el atasco
traffic lights el semáforo
trailer la caravana, el remolque
train el tren
trainee el aprendiz
trainers los zapatos de deporte
translate traducir
translator el traductor/ la traductora

travel agency la agencia de viajes
traveller's cheque el cheque de viaje
tray la bandeja
tree el árbol
trolley el carrito
trousers el pantalón
truck el camión
true cierto; *it's true* es verdad
try intentar
Tuesday martes
tunnel el túnel
turn (left/right) tuerza (a la izquierda/ a la derecha)
turn: it's my turn me toca a mí
tweezers las pinzas
twelve doce
twenty veinte
two dos
typewriter la máquina de escribir
tyre el neumático

U

ugly feo
umbrella el paraguas
uncle el tío
under ... debajo de ...
underground (railway) el metro
underpants los calzoncillos
understand entender; *I don't understand* no entiendo
underwear la ropa interior
United States Estados Unidos
university la universidad
unleaded sin plomo
until hasta
unusual poco común
up arriba; (upward) hacia arriba
urgent urgente
us: it's for us es para nosotros/nosotras; *give it to us* dénoslo
use el uso; (verb) usar; *it's no use* no sirve de nada
useful útil
usual corriente
usually en general

V

vacancies (rooms) habitaciones libres
vaccination la vacuna
vacuum cleaner la aspiradora
valley el valle

valve la válvula
vanilla la vainilla
vase el jarrón
veal la (carne de) ternera
vegetables la verdura
vegetarian vegetariano
vehicle el vehículo
very muy; *very much* mucho
vest la camiseta
vet el veterinario
video (tape) la cinta de vídeo; (film) el vídeo
video games los vídeojuegos
video recorder el (aparato de) vídeo
view la vista
viewfinder el visor de imagen
villa el chalet
village el pueblo
vinegar el vinagre
violin el violín
visit la visita; visitar (verb)
visiting hours las horas de visita
visitor el/la visitante
vitamin pills las vitaminas
vodka la vodka
voice la voz
voicemail la mensajería de voz

W

wait esperar; *wait!* ¡espere!
waiter el camarero; *waiter!* ¡camarero!
waiting room la sala de espera
waitress la camarera; *waitress!* ¡Oiga, por favor!
Wales Gales
walk (stroll) el paseo; (verb) andar; *to go for a walk* ir de paseo
wall la pared; (outside) el muro
wallet la cartera
want (verb) querer
war la guerra
wardrobe el armario
warm caliente; (weather) caluroso
was estaba/era
washing machine la zapatilla
washing powder el jabón de lavadora, el detergente
washing-up liquid el lavavajillas
wasp la avispa
watch el reloj; (verb) mirar

water el agua
waterfall la cascada
water heater
  el calentador (de agua)
wave la ola; (verb)
  agitar
wavy (hair) ondulado
we nosotros/nosotras
weather el tiempo
website la web site,
  el sitio web
wedding la boda
Wednesday miércoles
weeds las malas hierbas
week la semana
welcome (adj)
  bienvenido; (verb)
  dar la bienvenida;
  you're welcome
  no hay de qué
wellington boots
  las botas de agua
Welsh galés/galesa
were: you were
  (informal singular)
  eras/estabas, (formal
  singular) era/estaba;
  (informal plural)
  erais/estabais;
  (formal plural)
  eran/estaban; we
  were éramos/
  estábamos; they were
  eran/estaban
west el oeste
wet mojado
what? ¿qué?
wheel la rueda
wheel brace la llave de
  las tuercas
wheelchair la silla de
  ruedas

when? ¿cuándo?
where? ¿dónde?
whether si
which? ¿cuál?
whisky el whisky
white blanco
white coffee el café con
  leche
who? ¿quién?
why? ¿por qué?
wide ancho; 3 metres
  wide de tres metros
  de anchura
wife la mujer
wind el viento
window la ventana
windscreen el parabrisas
wine el vino
wine list la carta de
  vinos
wine merchant
  el vinatero
wing el ala
with con
without sin
witness el testigo
woman la mujer
wood (material)
  la madera
wool la lana
word la palabra
work el trabajo; (verb)
  trabajar; (to
  function) funcionar
worktop el mostrador
worse peor
worst (el) peor
wrapping paper
  el papel de envolver;
  (for presents)
  el papel de regalo
wrench la llave inglesa

wrist la muñeca
writing paper el papel
  de escribir
wrong equivocado

X, Y, Z

x-ray department
  el servicio de
  radiología
year el año
yellow amarillo
yes sí
yesterday ayer
yet todavía; not yet
  todavía no
yoghurt el yogur
you (informal
  singular) tú; (formal
  singular) usted;
  (informal plural,
  m/f) vosotros/
  vosotras; (formal
  plural) ustedes
young joven
your: your book
  (informal singular)
  tu libro; (formal
  singular) su libro;
  your shoes (informal
  singular) tus zapatos;
  (formal singular)
  sus zapato
yours: is this yours?
  (informal) ¿es tuyo
  esto?; (formal) ¿es suyo
  esto?
youth hostel el albergue
  juvenil
zip la cremallera
zoo el zoo

Dictionary
Spanish *to English*

The gender of Spanish nouns listed here is indicated by the abbreviations "(m)" and "(f)", for masculine and feminine. Plural nouns are followed by the abbreviations "(m pl)" or "(f pl)". Spanish adjectives (adj) vary according to the gender and number of the word they describe, and the masculine form is shown here. In general, adjectives that end in **-o** adopt an **-a** ending in the feminine form, and those that end in **-e** usually stay the same. For the plural form, an **-s** is added.

A

a *to*; a América *to America*; a la estación *to the station*; al médico *to the doctor*; a las tres *at 3 o'clock*

abanico (m) *fan (handheld)*

abierto *open* (adj)

abogado/abogada (m/f) *lawyer*

abrebotellas (m) *bottle opener*

abrelatas (m) *can opener*

abrigo (m) *coat*

abril *April*

abrir *to open*

abuela (f) *grandmother*

abuelo (m) *grandfather*

abuelos (m pl) *grandparents*

aburrido *boring*

acaba de llegar *it's just arrived*

accidente (m) *accident*

aceite (m) *oil*; el aceite de oliva *olive oil*

aceituna (f) *olive*

acelerador (m) *accelerator*

acera (f) *pavement*

acondicionador (m) *conditioner* (hair)

acuerdo: me acuerdo *I remember*; no me acuerdo *I don't remember*

adaptador (m) *adaptor*

adelantar *overtake* (car)

adiós *goodbye*

aduana (f) *customs*

aerodeslizador (m) *hovercraft*

aeropuerto (m) *airport*

afeitado (m) *shave*; afeitarse *to have a shave*

after-shave (m) *aftershave*

afueras (f pl) *suburbs*

agencia (f) *agency*

agencia de viajes (f) *travel agency*

agenda (f) *diary*

agitar *to wave*

agosto *August*

agradable *pleasant*

agradecer *to thank*

agua (m) *water*; el agua con gas *fizzy water*; el agua mineral *mineral water*; el agua potable *drinking water*; el agua sin gas *still water*

aguja (f) *needle*

ahora *now*; ¿y ahora qué? *what next?*

aire (m) *air*

aire acondicionado (m) *air conditioning*

ajedrez (m) *chess*

ajo (m) *garlic*

ajustado *tight*

ala (m) *wing*

albañil (m) *builder*

albaricoque (m) *apricot*

albergue juvenil (m) *youth hostel*

alcachofa (f) *artichoke*

alcohol (m) *alcohol*

alegre *glad*

alemán *German*

Alemania *Germany*

alérgico *allergic*

alfiler (m) *pin*

alfombra (f) *carpet; rug*

algo *something*

algodón (m) *cotton, cotton wool*

alguien *somebody*

alguna: en alguna parte *somewhere*

allí *there, over there*

almohada (f) *pillow*

alojamiento (m) *accommodation*

alquilar *to hire*

alto *high, tall, loud*

¡alto! *stop!*

amante (m/f) *lover*

amargo *bitter*

amarillo *yellow*

ambulancia (f) *ambulance*

América *America*

americano/americana (m/f) *American*

amigo/amiga (m/f) *friend*; amigo/amiga por correspondencia (m/f) *pen pal*

amontillado *medium* (sherry)

amor (m) *love*

ampliación (f) *enlargement*

ampolla (f) *blister*

análisis de sangre (m) *blood test*

andar *to walk*

andén (m) *platform*

anfiteatro (m) *lecture theatre*

anfitriona (f) *hostess*

anillo (m) *ring (jewellery)*

animal (m) *animal*; los animales de compañía/los animales domésticos *pets*

año (m) *year*

antes de ... *before ...*

anticonceptivo (m) *contraceptive*

anticongelante (m) *antifreeze*

anticuario (m) *antique shop*

antiséptico (m) *antiseptic*

aparcamiento (m) *car park*

aparcar *to park*; prohibido aparacar *no parking*

apartamento (m) *apartment*

apellido (m) *surname*

aperitivo (m) *aperitif*

apetito (m) *appetite*

aprender *learn*

aprendiz (m) *trainee*

apretón de manos (m) *handshake*

araña (f) *spider*

árbol (m) *tree*

árbol de levas (m) *camshaft*

arcón (m) *chest* (furniture)

arena (f) *sand*

Argelia *Algeria*

armario (m) *cupboard, wardrobe*

arreglar *repair*

arriba *up*; hacia arriba *upward*

arroyo (m) *stream* (small river)

arroz (m) *rice*

arte (m) *art*

artículos de punto (m pl) *knitwear*

artista (m/f) *artist*

asado *roasted*

ascensor (m) *lift*

asiento (m) *seat*; el asiento infantil *car seat* (for a baby/child)

asistenta (f) *cleaner*

asmático *asthmatic*

aspiradora (f) *vacuum cleaner*

aspirina (f) *aspirin*

atar *to tie*

atasco (m) *traffic jam*

aterrizar *to land*

ático (m) *attic*

atractivo *attractive* (offer)

audífono (m) *hearing aid*

auriculares (m pl) *headphones*

Australia *Australia*

australiano/australiana (m/f) *Australian*

autobús (m) *bus*; autobús del aeropuerto *airport bus*

autocaravana (f) *camper van*

automático *automatic*

autónomo/autónoma (m/f) *self-employed*

autopista (f) *motorway*

avería (f) (car) *breakdown*; he tenido una avería *I've had a breakdown*

aves (f pl) *poultry*

avión (m) *aircraft*

avispa (f) *wasp*

ayer *yesterday*

ayuda (f) *help*

ayudar *to help*

ayuntamiento (m) *town hall*

azúcar (m) *sugar*

azul *blue*

B

bacon (m) *bacon*

bailar *to dance*

baile (m) *dance*

bajarse *to get off* (bus etc) ; *to get out*

bajo *low, short*

balandro (m) *sailing boat*

balcón (m) *balcony*

Baleares: las (Islas) Baleares *Balearic Islands*

balón (m) *football* (ball); el balón de playa *beach ball*

baloncesto (m) *basketball*

bañador (m) *bathing suit, swimming trunks*

banco (m) *bank*

banda (f) *band* (musicians)

bandeja (f) *tray*

bandera (f) *flag*

baño (m) *bath, bathroom, toilet* (room in a house); darse un baño *to have a bath*; el traje de baño *bathing suit*

bar (m) *bar* (drinks)

baraja (f) *deck of cards*

barato *inexpensive*

barba (f) *beard*

barbacoa (f) *barbecue*

barca (f) *small boat*; la barca de remos *rowing boat*

barco (m) *boat, ship*

barra de labios (f) *lipstick*

bastante *enough, quite, fairly*

basura (f) *litter, rubbish*

batería (f) *battery* (car)

bebé (m) *baby*

beber *to drink*; ¿quiere beber algo? *would you like something to drink?*

bebida (f) *drink*

beige *beige*

beneficios (m pl) *profits*

berenjenas (f pl) *aubergines*

biblioteca (f) *library*

bicicleta (f) *bicycle*; la bicicleta de montaña *mountain bike*

bien *good*; te sienta bien *it suits you*

bienvenido *welcome*

bigote (m) *moustache*

billete (m) *fare, ticket* (train etc); billete de ida y vuelta (m) *return ticket*

billete de banco (m) *banknote*

bizcocho (m) *sponge cake*

blanco *white*

blando *soft*

bloc (m) *notepad*

bloque de oficinas (m) *office block*

blusa (f) *blouse*

boca (f) *mouth*

bocadillo (m) *sandwich*

boda (f) *wedding*

bodega (f) *cellar*

bolígrafo (m) *ballpoint pen*

bollo (m) *roll* (bread)

bolsa (f) *bag, packet* (sweets, crisps); la bolsa de basura *bin liner*; la bolsa de plástico *plastic bag*

bolsillo (m) *pocket*

bolso (m) *handbag*

bombilla (f) *light bulb*

bonito *nice, pretty, attractive* (object)

bordado (m) *embroidery*

borde (m) *edge, border, side*

borracho *drunk*

bosque (m) *forest*

bota (f) *boot*

botas de agua (f pl) *wellington boots*

botella (f) *bottle*

botón (m) *button*

brazo (m) *arm*

bridge (m) *bridge* (game)

británico/británica (m/f) *British*

brocha (f) *paint brush*

broche (m) *brooch*

broma (f) *joke*

bronceado *suntanned*

broncearse *suntan: to get a suntan*

buenas noches *good evening*

buenas tardes *good afternoon*

bueno *good, good to eat, tasty*

buenos días *good morning*

bufanda (f) *scarf*

buzón (m) *postbox*

C

cabeza (f) *head*

cabina telefónica (f) *phone booth*

cable alargador (m) *extension cord*

cacahuetes (m pl) *peanuts*

cada *every, each*; viente euros cada uno *20 euros each*

café (m) *café, coffee;*
el café con leche
white coffee; el café
instantáneo *instant*
coffee; el café solo
espresso
caja (f) *box; check-out;*
la caja de bombones
box of chocolates;
la caja de cambios
gearbox
cajero (m) *cashier;*
el cajero automático
ATM, cashpoint
cajetilla (f) *packet*
(cigarettes)
calambre (m) *cramp*
calcetines (m pl) *socks*
calculadora (m)
calculator
calefacción (f) *heating;*
la calefacción central
central heating
calentador (de agua)
(m) *water heater*
calidad (f) *quality*
caliente *warm*
callado *quiet* (person)
calle (f) *street;* la calle
principal *main road*
caluroso *warm*
(weather)
calzoncillos (m pl)
underpants
cama (f) *bed*
cámara de fotos (f)
camera
cámara neumática (f)
inner tube
camarera (f) *waitress*
camarero (m) *waiter;*
¡camarero! *waiter!*
cambiar *to change*
(money)
cambiarse *to change*
(clothes)
cambio (m) *change*
(money); *exchange*
rate
camino (m) *path*
camión (m) *truck*
camisa (f) *shirt*
camiseta (f) *vest*
camisón (m)
nightgown
campana (f) *bell*
(church)
camping (m) *campsite*
camping-gas (m)
camping gas
campo (m) *countryside,*
field
Canadá *Canada*
canadiense *Canadian*
canal (m) *canal*
Canarias: las (Islas)
Canarias *Canaries*
canción (f) *song*
candado (m) *padlock*
cangrejo (m) *crab*
cansado *tired*

cantar *to sing*
capazo (m) *crib*
capó (m) *bonnet* (car)
cara (f) *face*
caramelos (m) *sweets*
caravana (f) *trailer*
carburador (m)
carburetor
cardenal (m) *bruise*
cargador (m) *charger*
carne (f) *meat*
carne de cerdo (f) *pork*
carne de vaca (f) *beef*
carnet de conducir (m)
driving licence
carnicería (f) *butcher's*
caro *expensive*
carpintero (m)
carpenter
carretera (f) *road*
carrito (m) *trolley*
carta (f) *letter* (mail);
menu; la carta de
vinos (f) *wine list*
cartera (f) *purse,*
briefcase, wallet
carterista (m)
pickpocket
cartero (m) *postman*
casa (f) *house, home;*
en casa *at home*
casado *married*
cascada (f) *waterfall*
casi *almost*
cassette (f) *cassette*
castaño *brown* (hair)
castañuelas (f pl)
castanets
castellano *Castilian*
Castilla *Castile*
castillo (m) *castle*
Cataluña *Catalonia*
catedral (f) *cathedral*
catedrático (m)
professor
católico *Catholic* (adj)
catorce *fourteen*
cazo (m) *saucepan*
cebo (m) *bait*
cebolla (f) *onion*
ceja (f) *eyebrow*
cementerio (m)
cemetery
cena (f) *dinner, supper,*
dinner party
cenicero (m) *ashtray*
centro (m) *centre; city*
centre; el centro
deportivo *sports*
centre; en el centro
middle: in the middle
cepillar el pelo *to brush*
hair
cepillo (m) *brush* (for
cleaning); el cepillo
del pelo *hair brush;*
el cepillo de dientes
toothbrush
cerca *near, close;* (f)
fence
cereza (f) *cherry*

cerilla (f) *match* (light)
cerrado *closed*
cerrar *to close*
cerrojo (m) *bolt* (on
door)
certificado (m)
certificate
cerveza (f) *beer*
césped (m) *lawn*
cesto (m) *basket*
chal (m) *shawl*
chalet (m) *villa*
champiñones (m pl)
mushrooms
champú (m) *shampoo*
chandal (m) *track suit*
chaparrón (m) *shower*
(rain)
chaqueta (f) *jacket*
charcutería (f)
delicatessen
charla (f) *talk*
cheque (m) *cheque;*
el cheque de viaje
traveller's cheque
chica (f) *girl*
chicle (m) *chewing gum*
chico (m) *boy*
chimenea (f) *chimney,*
fireplace
chincheta (f) *drawing*
pin
chiste (m) *joke* (funny
story)
chocolate (m) *chocolate*
chuleta (f) *chop* (food)
chupa-chups (m)
lollipop
ciclismo (m) *cycling*
ciclomotor (m) *moped*
ciego *blind* (cannot
see)
cielo (m) *sky*
cien *hundred*
ciencias (f pl) *science*
cierto *true*
cigalas (f pl) *crayfish*
cigarrillo (m) *cigarette*
cinco *five*
cincuenta *fifty*
cine (m) *cinema*
cinta (f) *cassette;* el cinta
de vídeo *video tape*
cinturón (m) *belt;* el
cinturón de seguridad
seat belt
cita (f) *appointment*
ciudad (f) *city, town;*
el centro ciudad *city*
centre
claro *clear* (water);
light (adj: not dark)
clase (f) *class; lesson*
clavo (m) *nail* (metal)
claxon (m) *horn* (car)
cliente (m) *client*
cobrador (m) *conductor*
(bus)
cobrar *to cash*
cocer *to cook, boil*
cocer al horno *to bake*

coche (m) *car*

coche-cama (m) *sleeper car*

cochecito (m) *pram*

cocina (f) *cooker; kitchen*

cocinero/cocinera (m/f) *cook*

coctel (m) *cocktail party*

código *code;* el código de la circulación *highway code;* el código postal *postcode*

codo (m) *elbow*

coger *catch;* coger el tren *to catch the train*

cojín (m) *cushion*

col (f) *cabbage*

cola (f) *line*

colada (f) *laundry (washed)*

colcha (f) *bedspread*

colchón (m) *mattress*

colchoneta (f) *air mattress*

colección (f) *collection (stamps etc)*

coliflor (f) *cauliflower*

collar (m) *collar (of animal)*

collar (m) *necklace; colour*

combinacíon (f) *slip (underwear)*

comedor (m) *dining room*

comer *to eat*

comida (f) *food, meal; lunch*

comida ligera (f) *snack*

comisaría (f) *police station*

como *like;* como éste *like this one*

¿cómo? *how?;* ¿cómo se llama usted? *what's your name?;* ¿cómo dice? *pardon?, what did you say?*

cómoda (f) *chest of drawers*

compañía aérea (f) *airline*

compartimento (m) *compartment*

completamente *completely*

complicado *complicated*

compra (f) *shopping*

comprar *to buy*

comprendo *I see*

compresas (f pl) *sanitary towels*

con *with*

coñac (m) *brandy*

concha (f) *shell*

concierto (m) *concert*

concurrido *crowded*

condón (m) *condom*

conducir *to drive*

conductor (m) *driver*

conejo (m) *rabbit*

conferencia (f) *conference;* la sala de conferencias *conference room*

congelador (m) *freezer*

congelados (m pl) *frozen foods*

conocer *to know (person, place)*

conserje (m) *porter (hotel)*

consulado (m) *consulate*

contable (m/f) *accountant*

contenedor de basura (m) *bin*

contento *happy*

contestador automático (m) *answering machine*

contra *against*

contraseña (f) *password*

contrato (m) *contract*

copa (f) *glass (for drinking)*

corazón (m) *heart*

corazones (m pl) *hearts (cards)*

corbata (f) *tie*

corcho (m) *cork*

cordero (m) *lamb*

cordones (de los zapatos) (m pl) *(shoe)laces*

correa (f) *lead*

correcto *right (correct)*

correo (m) *mail, post;* el correo certificado *registered post;* el correo electrónico *email*

Correos: (la oficina de) Correos (f) *post office*

correr *to run*

corrida de toros (f) *bullfight*

corriente *ordinary; usual*

cortadura (f) *cut*

cortar *to chop, cut*

cortauñas (m) *nail clippers*

corte de pelo (m) *haircut*

cortina (f) *curtain*

corto *short*

coser *to sew*

cosméticos (m pl) *cosmetics*

costar *to cost;* ¿cuánto cuesta? *what does it cost?*

crema (f) *cream (lotion)*

crema de zapatos (f) *shoe polish*

cremallera (f) *zip*

creo que ... *I think that ...*

crepes (f pl) *pancakes*

crisis nerviosa (f) *nervous breakdown*

cristal (m) *glass (material)*

crucero (m) *cruise*

cuaderno (m) *notebook*

cuadrado *square (adj)*

¿cuál? *which?*

cualquiera de ellos *either of them*

¿cuándo? *when?*

¿cuánto cuesta? *what does it cost?, how much is it?*

¿cuántos años tiene? *how old are you?*

cuarenta *forty*

cuarto (m) *quarter, room;* (adj) *fourth*

cuarto de baño (m) *bathroom*

cuarto de estar (m) *living room, lounge*

cuatro *four*

cubo (m) *bucket;* el cubo de la basura *dustbin*

cucaracha (f) *cockroach*

cuchara (f) *spoon*

cuchillas de afeitar (f pl) *razor blades*

cuchillo (m) *knife*

cuello (m) *neck, collar*

cuenco (m) *bowl*

cuenta (f) *bill*

cuerda (f) *string; rope*

cuerno (m) *horn (animal)*

cuero (m) *leather*

cuerpo (m) *body*

cueva (f) *cave*

¡cuidado! *be careful!*

cumpleaños (m) *birthday*

cuna (f) *cot*

cura (m) *priest*

curry (m) *curry*

D

dar *give;* dar la bienvenida *to welcome*

de *of;* de algún modo *somehow;* de ida *single (ticket)*

debajo de *below, under*

decir *say;* ¿qué ha dicho? *what did you say?;* ¿cómo se dice ...? *how do you say ...?*

declaración (f) *statement*

dedo (m) *finger*

delante de *in front of*

...delgado *thin*

demasiado *too (excessively)*

démelo *give it to me*

dentadura postiza (f)
dentures, false teeth

dentista (m/f) dentist

denuncia (f) police report

departamento (m)
department

deporte (m) sport

derecho (m) law,
justice; no hay derecho
it's not fair; (adj)
right (not left)

desayuno (m) breakfast

descansar to rest

descuento (m) discount

desmayarse to faint

desodorante (m)
deodorant

despacho (m) office
(room)

despegue (m) take off

despertador (m) alarm
clock

después then (after);
después de ... after ...

destornillador (m)
screwdriver

detergente (m)
washing powder

detrás de ... behind ...

devolver to return (give
back); to be sick
(vomit)

día (m) day; el día de
fiesta public holiday

diabético diabetic

diamantes (m pl)
diamonds

diarrea (f) diarrhoea

diccionario (m)
dictionary

diciembre December

diecinueve nineteen

dieciocho eighteen

dieciséis sixteen

diecisiete seventeen

diente (m) tooth

diesel diesel (adj:
engine)

diez ten

diferente different

difícil difficult

dígame hello (on
phone)

dinero (m) money,
cash; no tengo dinero
I have no money

dirección (f) address

director/directora (m/f)
manager (hotel);
conductor (orchestra)

disco (m) record
(music)

disco compacto (m)
compact disc

discoteca (f) nightclub

diseñador/diseñadora
(m/f) designer

disponible available

distancia distance; ¿qué
distancia hay a ...?
how far is it to ...?

distinto separate,
different (adj); ¡eso es
distinto! that's
different!; quería otro
distinto I'd like a
different one

diversiones (f pl)
entertainment

divertido; (odd) raro
funny

divorciado divorced

doce twelve

documento (m)
document

dólar (m) dollar

dolor (m) ache, pain;
el dolor de cabeza
headache; el dolor de
estómago stomach-
ache; el dolor de
muelas toothache

domingo Sunday

¿dónde? where?;
¿dónde está ...? where
is ...?

dónut (m) doughnut

dormir to sleep

dormitorio (m) bedroom

dos two; los dos both

ducha (f) shower (bath)

dulce sweet (adj: not
sour)

dunas (f pl) sand dunes

durante during

duro hard (not soft)

duty-free (m) duty-free
shop

E

echar al correo to post

echar el cerrojo to bolt

edificio (m) building

edredón (m) duvet

eje (m) axle

ejecutivo (m) executive

ejemplo (m) example;
por ejemplo for
example

él he, him, the (m);
es para él it's for him

elástico elastic

electricidad (f)
electricity

electricista (m/f)
electrician

eléctrico electric

ella she, her, the (f);
es para ella it's for her

ellos/ellas they, them;
es para ellos/ellas
it's for them

email (m) email; la
dirección de email
email address

embajada (f) embassy

embarazada pregnant

embarazoso
embarrassing

emergencia (f)
emergency

empaste (m) filling (in
tooth)

empezar to start

empleado (m) employee

empujar to push

en on, at, in; en inglés
in English; en el hotel
in the hotel; en
Barcelona in
Barcelona; en Correos
at the post office; en su
casa at your place

encaje (m) lace

encantado/encantada
(m/f) pleased to meet
you

encargado (m) caretaker

encendedor (m) lighter

encendido (m) ignition

enchufe (m) plug
(electrical)

encima de ... over ...

encuentro (m) meeting;
no me encuentro bien
I don't feel well

enero January

enfermo/enferma (m/f)
nurse

enfrente de opposite;
enfrente del hotel
opposite the hotel

¡enhorabuena!
congratulations!

ensalada (f) salad

entender to understand;
no entiendo I don't
understand

entonces then, so

entrada (f) entrance,
ticket (theatre etc)

entrantes (m pl) starters

entre ... between ...

entrega (f) delivery

enviar por fax to fax

epiléptico epileptic

equipaje (m) luggage;
el equipaje de mano
hand luggage

equipo de música (m)
music system

equivocación (f)
mistake

equivocado wrong

era you were (formal):
it/he/she was

éramos we were

eran they were

eras you were
(informal)

eres you are (informal)

es you are (formal)

es it/he/she is

escalera (f) staircase;
la escalera mecánica
escalator; las escaleras
stairs

escarcha (f) frost

escocés/escocesa
(m/f) Scottish

Escocia Scotland

escopeta (f) gun (rifle)

escuela (f) *school*

ese/esa *that;* ese autobús *that bus;* ese hombre *that man;* esa mujer *that woman;* ¿qué es eso? *what's that?*

ése/ésa *that, that one;* esmalte de uñas (m) *nail polish*

esos/esas *those, those ones;* esos hombres *those men;* esas mujeres *those women*

espalda (f) *back* (body)

España *Spain*

español/española (m/f) *Spanish, Spaniard*

especialidad (f) *field of study*

espejo (m) *mirror*

esperar *to wait;* ¡espere! *wait!*

espinacas (f pl) *spinach*

espuma de afeitar (f) *shaving foam*

espuma moldeadora (f) *mousse* (for hair)

esquina (f) *corner* (of street)

esquís (m pl) *skis*

está *you are* (formal)

está *it/he/she is*

esta noche *tonight*

estaba *it/he/she was; you were* (formal)

estábamos *we were*

estaban *they were*

estabas *you were* (informal)

estaca (f) *tent peg*

estación (f) *station;* la estación de autobuses *bus station;* la estación de esquí *ski resort;* la estación de metro *metro station*

Estados Unidos *United States*

estamos *we are*

están *they are*

estanco (m) *tobacconist*

estaquilla (f) *tent peg*

estás *you are* (informal)

estatua (f) *statue*

este *east;* el Este *the East*

éste/ésta *this, this one;* este hombre *this man;* esta mujer *this woman;* ¿qué es esto? *what's this?;* éste es el señor ... *this is Mr ...*

estómago (m) *stomach*

estos/estas *these, these ones;* estos hombres *these men;* estas mujeres *these women;* éstos son míos *these are mine*

estoy *I am*

estrecho *narrow* (adj)

estrella (f) *star*

estudiante (m/f) *student*

estufa (f) *heater*

estúpido *stupid*

etiqueta (f) *label*

evidente *clear* (obvious)

excelente *excellent*

exceso de equipaje (m) *excess baggage*

excursión (f) *excursion, tour*

exposición (f) *exhibition*

externa *external*

extintor (m) *fire extinguisher*

extranjero/extranjera (m/f) *foreigner*

F

fácil *easy*

factor de protección (m) *protection factor (SPF)*

factura (f) *invoice*

facturación (f) *check-in*

facturar *to check in*

falda (f) *skirt*

falta, no hace falta *there's no need*

familia (f) *family*

fan (m) *fan* (enthusiast)

fantástico *fantastic*

farmacia (f) *chemist*

faros (m pl) *headlights*

fax (m) *fax*

febrero *February*

¡felicidades! *happy birthday!*

feliz *happy*

feo *ugly*

feria (f) *fair, trade fair*

ferretería (f) *hardware store*

ferrocarril (m) *railway*

ferry (m) *ferry*

fiebre (f) *temperature, fever;* la fiebre del heno *hay fever*

fiesta (f) *party* (celebration)

filete (m) *steak*

filtro (m) *filter*

fin (m) *end;* ¡por fin! *at last!*

final (m) *end*

fino *dry* (sherry)

flash (m) *flash* (camera)

flauta (f) *flute*

flequillo (m) *fringe* (hair)

flexo (m) *angle-poise lamp*

flor (f) *flower*

folleto (m) *brochure, leaflet*

fonda (f) *inn*

fondo (m) *bottom*

fontanero/fontanera (m/f) *plumber*

foto(grafía) (f) *photograph*

fotocopiadora (f) *photocopier*

fotografiar *to photograph*

fotógrafo (m) *photographer*

fotómetro (m) *light meter*

frambuesa (f) *raspberry*

francés *French*

Francia *France*

fregadero (m) *sink*

freír *to fry*

frenar *to brake*

freno (m) *brake;* el freno de emergencia *emergency brake;* el freno de mano *handbrake*

fresas (f pl) *strawberries*

fresco *cool*

frigorífico (m) *fridge*

frío *cold* (adj); *I'm cold* tengo frío

frito *fried*

frontera (f) *border* (between countries)

fruta (f) *fruit*

fuego (m) *fire;* los fuegos artificiales *fireworks*

fuel-oil *diesel* (oil)

fuente (f) *fountain*

fuera *outside*

fuerte *strong*

fumar *to smoke*

funcionar *to work* (function)

fútbol (m) *football* (game)

G

gabardina (f) *raincoat*

gafas (f pl) *glasses;* las gafas de sol *sunglasses*

galería de arte (f) *art gallery*

Gales *Wales*

galés/galesa *Welsh*

galleta (f) *biscuit*

gambas (f pl) *prawns*

ganga (f) *bargain*

garage (m) *garage* (for parking)

garantía (f) *guarantee*

garantizar *to guarantee*

garganta (f) *throat*

gas para el encendedor (m) *lighter fuel*

gasolina (f) *petrol*

gasolinera (f) *petrol station*

gato (m) *cat*

gay *gay* (homosexual)

gel (m) *gel* (hair); el gel de ducha *shower gel*

gemelos (m pl) *cuff links*

general: en general *usually*

gente (f) *people*

gerente (m/f) *manager*

Gibraltar *Gibraltar*

ginebra (f) *gin*

gobierno (m) *government*

Golfo de Vizcaya (m) *Bay of Biscay*

goma (f) *rubber band*; *rubber* (material)

goma de borrar (f) *eraser*

gordo *fat* (adj)

gorra (f) *cap* (hat)

gorro (m) *woollen hat*

gotas (f pl) *drops*

gracias *thank you*

Gran Bretaña *Great Britain*

grande *big, large*

grandes almacenes (m pl) *department store*

granja (f) *farm*

granjero (m) *farmer*

grapadora (f) *stapler*

grasa (f) *fat* (meat etc)

gratis *free* (no charge)

grifo (m) *tap*

gris *grey*

gritar *to shout*

grosellas negras (f pl) *blackcurrants*

grueso *thick*

grupo (m) *party* (group)

guantes (m pl) *gloves*

guapo *attractive, beautiful, handsome* (person)

guerra (f) *war*

guía (m/f) *guide*; la guía telefónica *phone book*; la guía turística *guide book*

guisantes (m pl) *peas*

guisar *to cook*

guitarra (f) *guitar*

gustar *like*: me gusta ... *I like ...*; me gusta nadar *I like swimming*

H

habitación (f) *room*; la habitación doble *double room*; la habitación individual *single room*; habitaciones libres *vacancies*

hablar *to talk*; ¿habla ...? *do you speak ...?*; no hablo ... *I don't speak ...*

hacer *to do, make*; hacer auto-stop *to hitchhike*; hacer footing *to jog*; hacer punto *to knit*;

hacer transbordo *to change* (trains etc); hace sol *it's sunny*

hacha (m) *axe*

hacia abajo *down*

hambre *hungry*; tengo hambre *I'm hungry*

hamburguesa (f) *hamburger*

hámster (m) *hamster*

harina (f) *flour*

hasta *until*

hay... *there is/are...* ; ¿hay ...? *is/are there ...?*

helado (m) *ice cream*

hepatitis (f) *hepatitis*

herida (f) *injury*

hermana (f) *sister*

hermano (m) *brother*

hervido *boiled*

hervidor de agua (m) *kettle*

hervir *to boil* (water)

hidroaleta (f) *hydrofoil*

hielo (m) *ice*

hierba (f) *grass*

hierro (m) *iron* (material)

hígado (m) *liver*

higo (m) *fig*

hija (f) *daughter*

hijastra (f) *stepdaughter*

hijastro (m) *stepson*

hijo (m) *son*

hincha (m) *football fan*

historia (f) *history*

hobby (m) *hobby*

hoguera (f) *campfire*

hoja (f) *leaf, sheet* (of paper)

hojalata (f) *tin*

hola *hello*

hombre (m) *man*

hombro (m) *shoulder*

homeopatía (f) *homeopathy*

honrado *honest*

hora (f) *hour*; ¿qué hora es? *what's the time?*

horario (m) *timetable*; el horario de apertura *opening times*

horca (f) *garden fork*

horno (m) *oven*

horrible *awful, horrible*

hospital (m) *hospital*

hoy *today*

hueso (m) *bone*

huevo (m) *egg*

húmedo *damp*

humo (m) *smoke*

I

idioma (m) *language*

iglesia (f) *church*

imperdible (m) *safety pin*

imposible *impossible*

impreso de solicitud (m) *application form*

impresora (f) *printer*

incendio (m) *fire* (blaze)

incluido *included*

indigestión *indigestion*

infección (f) *infection*

información (f) *information*

informe (m) *report*

ingeniería (f) *engineering*

Inglaterra *England*

inglés/inglesa *English*

inhalador (m) *inhaler* (for asthma etc)

inmediatamente *immediately*

insecto (m) *insect*

insolación (f) *sunstroke*

insomnio (m) *insomnia*

instrumento musical (m) *musical instrument*

intentar *to try*

interesante *interesting*

intermitente (m) *indicator*

internet (m) *internet*

interpretar *to interpret*

intérprete (m/f) *interpreter*

interruptor (m) *switch*

intoxicación alimenticia (f) *food poisoning*

invitación (f) *invitation*

invitada (f) *guest*

inyección (f) *injection*

ir *to go*; ir a esquiar *to go skiing*; ir de compras *to go shopping*

Irlanda *Ireland*; Irlanda del Norte *Northern Ireland*

irlandés/irlandesa *Irish*

isla (f) *island*

Italia *Italy*

italiano/italiana (m/f) *Italian*

izquierdo *left* (not right)

J

jabón (m) *soap*; el jabón de lavadora *washing powder*

jamón (m) *ham*

jarabe (m) *syrup*

jardín (m) *garden*

jarrita (f) *mug*

jarrón (m) *vase*

jaula (f) *cage*

jazz (m) *jazz*

jefe (m) *manager*

jengibre (m) *ginger* (spice)

jerez (m) *sherry*

jeringuilla (f) *syringe*

jersey (m) *sweater*

joven *young*

joyería (f) *jeweller's*
judías (f pl) *beans*
jueves *Thursday*
jugar *to play*
juguete (m) *toy*
julio *July*
junio *June*
junto a *near*; junto a la puerta *near the door*; junto a la ventana *near the window*
juntos *together*

K, L

kilo (m) *kilo*
kilómetro (m) *kilometre*
kiosko de periódicos (m) *newsagent's*
la (f) *the*
laca (f) *hairspray*
lado de (f) *beside*
ladrón (m) *thief*
lago (m) *lake*
lámpara (f) *lamp*
lamparilla de noche (f) *bedside lamp*
lana (f) *wool*
langosta (f) *lobster*
lápiz (m) *pencil*
largo *long*
las (f pl) *the*
lata (f) *can* (tin)
lavabo (m) *basin* (sink)
lavandería automática (f) *laundrette*
lavavajillas (m) *dishwasher*
laxante (m) *laxative*
leche (f) *milk*; la leche limpiadora *cleansing milk* (for skin)
lechuga (f) *lettuce*
leer *to read*
lejía *bleach*
lejos *far, far away*
lengua (f) *tongue*
lente (f) *lens*; las lentes de contacto *contact lenses*; las lentes de contacto semi-rígidas *gas-permeable lenses*
lento *slow*
letra (f) *letter* (of alphabet)
levantarse *to get up* (rise)
libra (f) *pound* (sterling)
libre *free* (not engaged)
libre de impuestos *duty-free*
libro (m) *book*; el libro de frases *phrase book*
licor (m) *liqueur*
ligero *light* (adj: not heavy)
lima (f) *lime* (fruit)
lima de uñas (f) *nailfile*
límite de velocidad (m) *speed limit*

limón (m) *lemon*
limonada (f) *lemonade*
limpio *clean* (adj)
línea (f) *line* (phone etc)
linterna (f) *torch*
lista (f) *list*
listo *clever; ready*
literatura (f) *literature*
litro (m) *litre*
llamar por teléfono *to telephone*
llave (f) *key*; la llave de las tuercas *wheel brace*; la llave inglesa *wrench*
llegar *to arrive*
lleno *crowded, full*; estoy lleno *I'm full (up)*
llorar *to cry* (weep)
lluvia (f) *rain*
lo/la *it*
lo antes posible *as soon as possible*
loción *lotion* (f)· la loción anti mosquitos *insect repellent lotion*; la loción bronceadora *suntan lotion*
loco *mad*
lona impermeable (f) *groundsheet*
longitud (f) *length*
los (m pl) *the*
lo siento *I'm sorry*
luces de posición (f pl) *side lights*
lugar (m) *place, sight*; los lugares de interés de ... *the sights of ...*
luna (f) *moon*
lunes *Monday*
luz (f) *light*

M

madastra (f) *stepmother*
madera (f) *wood* (material)
madre (f) *mother*
maduro *ripe*
malas hierbas (f pl) *weeds*
maleta (f) *suitcase*
maletero (m) *boot* (car)
Mallorca *Majorca*
malo *bad, poor* (quality)
mama *Mum*
mañana *tomorrow*
mañana (f) *morning*; por la mañana *in the morning*
mandar *to send*
mandarina (f) *tangerine*
manga (f) *sleeve*
mano (f) *hand*
manta (f) *blanket, rug*
mantequilla (f) *butter*
manzana (f) *apple*
mapa (m) *map*

maquillaje (m) *make-up*
maquina cortacésped (f) *lawn mower*
máquina de escribir (f) *typewriter*
máquina de fotos (f) *camera*
mar (m) *sea*
marea (f) *tide*
mareado *faint, dizzy*
margarina (f) *margarine*
marido (m) *husband*
mariscos (m pl) *seafood, shellfish*
mármol (m) *marble*
marrón *brown*
Marruecos *Morocco*
martes *Tuesday*
martillo (m) *hammer*
marzo *March*
más *more*; más de ... *more than ...* ; más tarde *later*; algo más *something else*; alguien más *someone else*
mástil (m) *tent pole*
matrícula (f) *number plate*
mayo *may*
mecánico (m) *mechanic*
media pensión *half board*
medianoche *midnight*
medias (f pl) *tights, stockings*
medicina (f) *medicine*
médico/médica (m/f) *doctor*
medio *half*; media hora *half an hour*
mediodía (m) *midday, noon*
Mediterráneo: el Mediterráneo *Mediterranean*
medusa (f) *jellyfish*
mejillones (m pl) *mussels*
mejor *best/better*
melocotón (m) *peach*
melón (m) *melon*
menos *less*
mensaje (m) *message*
mensajería de voz (f) *voicemail*
menú (del día) (m) *set menu*
menudo: a menudo *often*
mercado (m) *market*
mermelada (f) *jam*; la mermelada de naranja *marmalade*
mes (m) *month*
mesa (f) *table*; la mesa de escritorio *desk*
mesilla de noche (f) *bedside table*
metro (m) *underground* (railway)

mi(s) *my*; mi libro *my book*; mis llaves *my keys*

microondas (m) *microwave*

miel (f) *honey*

miércoles *Wednesday*

mil *thousand*

minusválido *disabled*

minuto (m) *minute*

mío *mine*; es mío *it's mine*

mirar *to watch*

misa (f) *mass* (church)

mismo *same*; el mismo vestido *the same dress*; la misma gente *the same people*; lo mismo otra vez, por favor *same again, please*

mochila (f) *backpack*

moda (f) *fashion*

modem (m) *modem*

mojado *wet*

moneda (f) *coin*

monedero (m) *purse*

monitor (m) *monitor*

montaña (f) *mountain*

monte (m) *hill*

monumento (m) *monument*

morado *purple*

moras (f pl) *blackberries*

mordedura (f) *bite* (dog)

morder *to bite* (dog)

morir *to die*

mosaico (m) *mosaic*

mosca (f) *fly* (insect)

mosquito (m) *mosquito*

mostaza (f) *mustard*

mostrador (m) *worktop*; el mostrador de facturación *check-in desk*

motocicleta (f) *motorcycle*

motor (m) *engine* (motor)

motora (f) *motorboat*

mover *to move* (something); moverse *move oneself*; ¡no se mueva! *don't move!*

mucho *much/many, a lot*; mucho mejor *much better*; mucho más despacio *much slower*; no muchos *not many*

mudarse (de casa) *to move* (house)

muebles (m pl) *furniture*

muela (f) *back tooth*

muelle (m) *dock*; *spring* (mechanical)

muerto *dead*

mujer (f) *woman, wife*

muletas (f pl) *crutches*

muñeca (f) *wrist*

muro (m) *wall* (outside)

museo (m) *museum*

música (f) *music*; la música clásica *classical music*; la música folklórica *folk music*; la música pop *pop music*

músico (m) *musician*

muy *very*

N

nací en ... *I was born in ...*

nada *nothing*; no queda nada *there's nothing left*; no sirve de nada *it's no use*

nadar *to swim*

nadie *nobody*

naranja (f) *orange* (fruit); *orange* (adj)

nariz (f) *nose*

nata (f) *cream* (dairy)

natación (f) *swimming*

náuseas *sick*; tengo náuseas *I feel sick*

navaja (f) *penknife*

navidad (f) *Christmas*

necesario *necessary*

necesito ... *I need ...*

negar *to deny*

negativo (m) *negative* (photo)

negocio (m) *business*

negro *black*

neozelandés/neozeland esa *New Zealander*

neumático (m) *tyre*

ni ... ni ... *neither ... nor ...*

niebla (f) *fog*

nieta (f) *granddaughter*

nieto (m) *grandson*

nieve (f) *snow*

ninguno/ninguna: ninguno de ellos *neither of them*; en ninguna parte *nowhere*

niño/niña *child* (m/f); los niños *children*; el niño pequeño *baby*

no *no* (response), *not*; no hay de qué *you're welcome*; no importa *it doesn't matter*; no es/está ... *(s)he's not ...*

noche (f) *night*

nombre (m) *name*; el nombre de pila *first name*

norte (m) *north*

nosotros/nosotras *we, us*; es para nosotros/ nosotras *it's for us*

noticias (f pl) *news*

novela (f) *novel*

noventa *ninety*

novia (f) *girlfriend*

noviembre *November*

novio (m) *boyfriend*

nudista (m/f) *nudist*

nuestro *our*; es nuestro *it's ours*

Nueva Zelanda *New Zealand*

nueve *nine*

nuevo *new*

nuez (f) *nut* (fruit)

número (m) *number*; los números *figures*

nunca *never*

O

o *or*; o bien ... o ... *either ... or ...*

obra de teatro (f) *play* (theatre)

obturador (m) *shutter* (camera)

Océano Atlántico (m) *Atlantic Ocean*

ochenta *eighty*

ocho *eight*

octubre *October*

oculista (m/f) *optician*

ocupado *busy* (engaged); *occupied*

oeste (m) *west*

oficina (f) *office* (place); *branch* (of company); la oficina de objetos perdidos *lost property office*; la oficina de turismo *tourist office*

oído (m) *(inner) ear*

¡oiga, por favor! *excuse me!* (to get attention); *waiter/waitress!*

oír *to hear*

ojo (m) *eye*

ola (f) *wave*

oler *to smell*

olivo (m) *olive tree*

olor (m) *smell*

oloroso *sweet* (sherry)

olvidar *to forget*

once *eleven*

ondulado *wavy* (hair)

operación (f) *operation*

operadora (f) *operator*

oporto (m) *port* (drink)

orden del día (m) *agenda*

ordenador (m) *computer*

oreja *ear* (f)

órgano (m) *organ* (music)

oro (m) *gold*

orquesta (f) *orchestra*

oscuro *dark*; azul oscuro *dark blue*

ostra (f) *oyster*

otra vez *again*

otro *another; other*; el otro *the other one*; en otro sitio *somewhere else*

P

padrastro (m) *stepfather*
padre (m) *father*; los
 padres *parents*
pagar *to pay*; pagar al
 contado *to pay cash*
página (f) *page*
pago (m) *payment*
país (m) *country* (state)
pájaro (m) *bird*
pala (f) *spade*
palabra (f) *word*
palacio (m) *palace*
palanca de velocidades
 (f) *gear stick*
pálido *pale*
pan (m) *bread*
panadería (f) *bakery*
pañal (m) *nappy*; los
 pañales desechables
 disposable nappies
paño de cocina (m)
 dish cloth
pantalla (f) *lampshade,
 screen*
pantalón (m) *trousers*;
 los pantalones cortos
 shorts
pantis (m pl) *tights*
pañuelo (m) *headscarf*;
 los pañuelos de papel
 tissues
papá (m) *dad*
papel (m) *paper*;
 el papel de envolver/
 regalo *wrapping
 paper*; el papel de
 escribir *writing paper*;
 el papel higiénico
 toilet paper; los
 papeles de filtro
 filter papers
paquete (m) *package,
 packet, parcel*
par (m) *pair*
para *for*; es para mí *it's
 for me*; para el viernes
 by Friday; ¿para qué?
 what for?, para una
 semana *for a week*
parabrisas (m)
 windscreen
parachoques (m)
 bumper
parada (f) *stop* (bus);
 la parada de taxis
 taxi rank
parafina (f) *paraffin*
paraguas (m) *umbrella*
parar *to stop*
pared (f) *wall* (inside)
pariente (m) *relative*
parque (m) *park*
parrilla (f) *grill*
parte de atrás (f) *back*
 (not front)
parterre (m) *flowerbed*
partido (m) *match*
 (sport), *party*
 (political)

pasajero (m) *passenger*
pasaporte (m) *passport*;
 el pasaporte de
 animales *pet passport*
pasas (f pl) *raisins*
paseo (m) *walk, stroll*;
 ir de paseo *to go for a
 walk*
pasillo (m) *aisle,
 corridor*
paso elevado (m)
 flyover
pasta (f) *pasta*
pasta dentífrica (f)
 toothpaste
pastel (m) *cake* (small)
pastelería (f) *cake shop*
pastilla (f) *pill, tablet*;
 las pastillas de menta
 peppermints; las
 pastillas para la
 garganta *cough drops*
patata (f) *potato*;
 las patatas fritas
 chips, crisps
patinar *to skid*
patines para hielo
 (m pl) *ice skates*
peatón (m) *pedestrian*
pecho (m) *chest* (part
 of body)
pedazo (m) *piece*
pedido (m) *order*
pegamento (m)
 adhesive, glue
peinar *to comb*
peine (m) *comb*
película (f) *film, movie*;
 la película en color
 colour film
peligroso *dangerous*
pelo (m) *hair*
pelota (f) *ball*
peluquería (f)
 hairdresser;
 la peluquería de
 caballeros *barber*
pendientes (m pl)
 earrings
pensar *to think*; lo
 pensaré *I'll think
 about it*
pensión completa *full
 board*
peor *worse, worst*
pepino (m) *cucumber*
pequeño *little, small*
pera (f) *pear*
percha (f) *coat hanger*
¡perdón! *sorry!, excuse
 me!* (when sneezing
 etc)
perejil (m) *parsley*
perezoso *lazy*
perfecto *perfect*
perfume (m) *perfume*
periódico (m)
 newspaper
perla (f) *pearl*
permanente (f) *perm*
permiso (m) *licence*

pero *but*
perro (m) *dog*
persianas (f pl) *blinds*
pesado *heavy*
pesca (f) *fishing*
pescadería (f)
 fishmonger's
pescado (m) *fish*
 (food)
pescar: ir a pescar *to go
 fishing*
pez (m) *fish* (animal)
piano (m) *piano*
picadura (f) *bite* (by
 insect)
picaporte (m) *handle*
 (door)
picar *to bite* (insect)
picas (f pl) *spades*
 (cards)
picnic (m) *picnic*
pie (m) *foot*
pierna (f) *leg*
pijama (m) *pyjamas*
pila (f) *battery* (torch
 etc)
piloto (m) *pilot*
pimienta (f) *pepper*
 (spice)
pimiento (m) *pepper*
 (red, green)
pin (m) *PIN*
piña (f) *pineapple*
pinchazo (m) *puncture*
pino (m) *pine* (tree)
pintor (m) *decorator*
pintura (f) *paint*
pinza (f) *peg*; las pinzas
 tweezers
pipa (f) *pipe* (for
 smoking)
Pirineos: los Pirineos
 Pyrenees
piscina (f) *swimming
 pool*; la piscina
 municipal *public
 swimming pool*
piso (m) *apartment*;
 floor (storey)
pista (f) *runway*
pistola (f) *gun* (pistol)
pistón (m) *piston*
pizza (f) *pizza*
plancha (f) *iron* (for
 clothes); a la plancha
 grilled
planchar *to iron*
plano (m) *town map,
 town plan*; (adj) *flat,
 level*
planta (f) *plant*
planta baja (f) *ground
 floor*
plástico (m) *plastic*;
 el plástico para
 envolver *plastic wrap*
plata (f) *silver* (metal)
plátano (m) *banana*
plateado *silver
 (colour)*
platillo (m) *saucer*

plato (m) *plate*; el plato principal *main course*; los platos preparados *ready meals*

playa (f) *beach*

plaza (f) *pitch, square* (in town); la plaza de toros *bullring*

pluma (f) *pen*; la pluma estilográfica *fountain pen*

pobre *poor* (not rich)

poco *a little*; poco común *unusual*; poco hecho/pasado *rare* (steak)

poder *to be able*

policía (f) *police*

policía (m) *police officer*

política (f) *politics*

pollo (m) *chicken*

polvo (m) *powder*; los polvos *make-up powder*; los polvos de talco *talcum powder*

pomada (f) *ointment*

poner *to put*; ¿me pone ...? *can I have ...?*

poquito *a little*; sólo un poquito *just a little*

por *through, by, per*; por avión *by air mail*; por la noche *at night*; por noche *per night*; por todas partes *everywhere*

porcelana (f) *china(wear)*

por favor *please*

¿por qué? *why?*

porque *because*

portero (m) *caretaker*

Portugal *Portugal*

portugués *Portuguese*

posible *possible*

postal (f) *postcard*

póster (m) *poster*

postigo (m) *shutter* (window)

postre (m) *dessert*

precio (m) *price*; el precio de entrada (m) *admission charge*

precioso *beautiful* (object)

preferir *to prefer*

pregunta (f) *question*

presupuesto (m) *budget, estimate*

primavera (f) *spring* (season)

primer piso (m) *first floor*

primero *first*; de primera *first class*; primeros auxilios *first aid*

primo (m) *cousin*

prima (f) *cousin*

principiante (m/f) *beginner*

principio (m) *start, beginning*

prisa: tengo prisa *I'm in a hurry*

privado *private*

problema (m) *problem*

producto (m) *product*; los productos de belleza *beauty products*; los productos del hogar *household products*; los productos lácteos *dairy products*

profesión (f) *profession*

profesor/profesora (m/f) *teacher*

profesor/profesora de universidad (m/f) *lecturer* (university)

profundo *deep*

programa (m) *schedule*

prohibido *prohibited*

prometida (f) *fiancée*

prometido (m) *fiancé*

prometido/prometida (m/f) *engaged* (to be married)

propina (f) *tip* (money)

próximo *next*

prudente *careful*

prueba (f) *test*

público *public*

pueblo (m) *small town, village*

¿puede ...? *can you ...?*

puedo *I can*; no puedo *I can't*

puente (m) *bridge*

puerta (f) *door, gate*; la puerta de embarque *departure gate*

puerto (m) *harbour, port*

pulga (f) *flea*

pulpo (m) *octopus*

pulsera (f) *bracelet*

punta (f) *tip* (end)

puro (m) *cigar*

Q

que *than*

¿qué? *what?*

quemadura (f) *burn*

quemadura de sol (f) *sunburn*

quemar *to burn*

querer *to want, love*

querido *dear* (person)

queso (m) *cheese*

¿qué tal? *how are you?*

¿quién? *who?*

quinze *fifteen*

quirófano (m) *operating theatre*

quisquillas (f pl) *shrimps*

quizás *maybe, perhaps*

R

rábano (m) *radish*

radiador (m) *radiator*

radio (f) *radio*

rápido *fast, quick*

raro *rare* (uncommon)

rastrillo (m) *rake*

rata (f) *rat*

ratón (m) *mouse*

raya (f) *parting* (hair)

rebajas (f pl) *sale* (at reduced prices)

rebeca (f) *cardigan*

recado (m) *message*

recepción (f) *reception*

recepcionista (m/f) *receptionist*

receta (f) *prescription*

recibo (m) *receipt*

recobrar algo *to get something back*

recogida (f) *collection* (postal)

récord (m) *record* (sport etc)

recuerdo (m) *souvenir*

redondo *round* (circular)

regalo (m) *gift*; el regalo de cumpleaños *birthday present*

regla (f) *ruler* (for measuring)

reír *to laugh*

rejilla de equipajes (f) *luggage rack*

relajarse *to relax*

religión (f) *religion*

relleno (m) *filling* (in sandwich, cake)

reloj (m) *clock, watch*

remar *to row*

remolque (m) *trailer*

remos (m pl) *oars*

resaca (f) *hangover*

reserva (f) *reservation*

reservar *to book*

resfriado (m) *cold* (illness); tengo un resfriado *I have a cold*

respirar *to breathe*

restaurante (m) *restaurant*

resto (m) *rest, remainder*

retrasado *delayed*; el autobús se ha retrasado *the bus is late*

reunión (f) *meeting*

revelar *to develop* (film)

revista (f) *magazine*

rico *rich*

rímel (m) *mascara*

rincón (m) *corner* (of room)

riñón (m) *kidney*

río (m) *river*

rizos (m pl) *curls*

robar *steal*; lo han robado *it's been stolen*

robo (m) *robbery*
roca (f) *rock* (stone)
rock (m) *rock* (music)
rodilla (f) *knee*
rojo *red*
ron (m) *rum*
ropa (f) *clothes*; la ropa
de cama (f) *bed linen*;
la ropa interior
underwear; la ropa
sucia *laundry* (dirty)
rosa (adj) *pink*
rosa (f) *rose*
roto *broken*
rotonda (f) *roundabout*
rotulador (m) *felt-tip pen*
roulotte (f) *caravan*
rubí (m) *ruby* (stone)
rubio *blond(e)* (adj)
rueda (f) *wheel*;
la rueda pinchada
flat tyre
rugby (m) *rugby*
ruidoso *noisy*
ruinas (f pl) *ruins*
rulos (m pl) *curlers*

S

sábado *Saturday*
sábana (f) *sheet*
(bedding)
saber *to know* (fact);
no sé *I don't know*
sabor (m) *flavour*
sacacorchos (m)
corkscrew
sacapuntas (m) *pencil
sharpener*
sacar *to bring out*
saco de dormir (m)
sleeping bag
sal (f) *salt*
sala de espera (f)
waiting room
sala de pediatría (f)
children's ward
salchicha (f) *sausage*
salida (f) *exit,
departure*; las salidas
departures; la salida
de emergencia
emergency exit
salmón (m) *salmon*
salón (m) *lounge*
(in hotel)
salsa (f) *sauce*
¡salud! *cheers!* (toast)
sandalias (f pl) *sandals*
sangre (f) *blood*
sartén (f) *frying pan*
sauna (f) *sauna*
secador (de pelo) (m)
hairdryer
seco *dry*
sed *thirsty*; tengo sed
I'm thirsty
seda (f) *silk*
segundo (m) *second*
(noun; adj); de
segunda *second class*

seguro (m) *insurance*;
(adj) *sure, safe* (not
dangerous)
seis *six*
sello (m) *stamp*
selva *rainforest*
semáforo (m) *traffic
lights*
semana (f) *week*;
la semana pasada
last week; la semana
que viene *next week*
seminario (m) *seminar*
semi-seco *medium-dry*
(wine)
señal (f) *deposit*
sencillo *simple*
senderismo (m) *hiking*
señor *Mr, sir*
señora *Mrs, madam*
señorita *Miss*
separado *separated*
septiembre *September*
ser *to be*
serio *serious*
seropositivo *HIV
positive*
servicio (m) *service,
department*; el servicio
de habitaciones *room
service*; el servicio de
radiología *x-ray
department*; el servicio
de urgencias
emergency department
servicios (m pl)
toilets (in public
establishment); los
servicios de caballeros
men's toilets; los
servicios de señoras
women's toilets
servilleta (f) *napkin*
sesenta *sixty*
setas (f pl) *mushrooms*
setenta *seventy*
seto (m) *hedge*
si *if, whether*
sí *yes*
Sida (m) *AIDS*
siempre *always*
siete *seven*
significar: ¿qué significa
esto? *what does this
mean?*
siguiente *next*
silla (f) *chair*; la silla de
ruedas *wheelchair*
sillita de ruedas (f)
stroller, pushchair
simpático *friendly*
sin *without*; sin plomo
unleaded
sinagoga (f) *synagogue*
sitio (m) *room, space*;
el sitio web *website*
sobre (m) *envelope*
sobre todo *especially*
sobrina (f) *niece*
sobrino (m) *nephew*
soda *soda water*

sofa (m) *sofa*
sofocante *close, stuffy*
sol (m) *sun*
solo *alone*; yo solo *by
myself*
sólo *just, only*
soltero/soltera (m/f)
single (unmarried)
solución limpiadora (f)
soaking solution (for
contact lenses)
sombrero (m) *hat*
sombrilla (f) *sunshade*
somnífero (m) *sleeping
pill*
somos *we are*
son *they are*
sonreír *to smile*
sonrisa (f) *smile*
sopa (f) *soup*
sordo *deaf*
sostén (m) *bra*
sótano (m) *basement*
soy *I am*; soy de ...
I come from ...
spray (m) *inhaler* (for
asthma etc); el spray
antipulgas *flea spray*
su(s) *its/hers/his/your*
(formal); ¿es suyo
esto? *is this yours?*
subirse *to get in, get on*
(of train, bus etc)
sucio *dirty*
sudadera (f)
sweatshirt
Sudamérica *South
America*
sudar *to sweat*
sudor (m) *sweat*
suelo (m) *floor*; el
suelo aislante
groundsheet
sueño (m) *sleep*
suerte (f) *luck*; ¡suerte!
good luck!
supermercado (m)
supermarket
suplemento (m)
supplement
supositorio (m)
suppository
sur (m) *south*

T

tabaco (m) *tobacco*
tabla de windsurfing (f)
sailboard
tableta de chocolate (f)
bar of chocolate
tacón (m) *heel* (shoe)
taller (m) *garage* (for
repairs)
talón (m) *heel* (foot)
talonario de cheques
(m) *chequebook*
también *too* (also)
tampones (m pl)
tampons
tan *so*; tan bueno *so good*

tanto: no tanto *not so much*; tanto ... como ... *both ... and ...*

tapiz (m) *tapestry*

tapón (m) *cap* (bottle), *plug* (sink)

taquilla (f) *box office, ticket office*

tarde (f) *evening*; (adj) *late*; *it's getting late* se está haciendo tarde

tarifa (f) *fare*

tarjeta (f) *card*; la tarjeta de banco *bank card*; la tarjeta de crédito *credit card*; la tarjeta de embarque *boarding pass*; la tarjeta de vista *business card*; la tarjeta telefónica *phonecard*

tarta (f) *cake* (large)

taxi (m) *taxi*

taza (f) *cup*

té (m) *tea*

techo (m) *ceiling*

teclado (m) *keyboard*

técnico (m) *technician*

tejado (m) *roof*

tejanos (m pl) *jeans*

tela (f) *material* (cloth)

teleférico (m) *cable car*

teléfono (m) *telephone*; el teléfono móvil *mobile phone*

televisión (f) *television*; la televisión por cable *cable TV*

temperatura (f) *temperature*

temprano *early*

tenedor (m) *fork*

tener *to have*; tengo *I have*; no tengo *I don't have*; ¿tiene? *do you have?*; tengo que irme *I have to go*; tengo calor *I feel hot*; tengo que ... *I must ...*

teñir *to bleach* (hair)

tenis (m) *tennis*

tenue *faint* (unclear)

tercero *third*

terminal (f) *terminal*

ternera (f) *veal*

terraza (f) *terrace*

testigo (m) *witness*

tía (f) *aunt*

tiempo (m) *time, weather*

tienda (f) *shop*; la tienda de comestibles *grocer's*; la tienda de discos *record store*

tienda (de campaña) (f) *tent*

¿tiene ...? *do you have ...?*

tierra (f) *land, soil*

tijeras (f pl) *scissors*

timbre (m) *bell* (door)

tinta (f) *ink*

tinto *red* (wine)

tintorería (f) *dry cleaner*

tío (m) *uncle*

tirantes (m pl) *braces*

tirar *to pull*

tirita (f) *plaster*

toalla (f) *towel*

toallitas para bebé (f pl) *baby wipes*

tobillo (m) *ankle*

toca: me toca a mí *it's my turn*

tocadiscos (m) *record player*

tocar *to feel* (touch)

todavía *yet*; todavía no *not yet*

todo *everything, all*; eso es todo *that's all*

todos *everyone*

todos los días *every day*

tomar *to take*; tomar el sol *to sunbathe*

tomate (m) *tomato*

tónica (f) *tonic*

torero (m) *bullfighter*

tormenta (f) *storm*

tornillo (m) *screw*

toro (m) *bull*

torre (f) *tower*

tortilla (f) *omelette*

tos (f) *cough*

toser *to cough*

tostada (f) *toast*

trabajar *to work* (job)

trabajo (m) *job, work*

tractor (m) *tractor*

tradición (f) *tradition*

traducir *to translate*

traductor/traductora (m/f) *translator*

traer *to fetch*

tráfico (m) *traffic*

traje (m) *suit* (clothing)

tranquilo *quiet*

trapo del polvo (m) *duster*

trasero (m) *bottom* (part of body)

tréboles (m pl) *clubs* (cards)

trece *thirteen*

treinta *thirty*

tren (m) *train*

tres *three*

triste *sad*

tú *you* (informal)

tu(s) *your* (informal); tu libro *your book*; tus zapatos *your shoes*; ¿es tuyo esto? *is this yours?*

tubería (f) *pipe* (for water)

tubo de escape (m) *exhaust*

tuerca (f) *nut* (for bolt)

tuerza (a la izquierda/derecha) *turn (left/right)*

túnel (m) *tunnel*

turismo (m) *sightseeing*

turista (m/f) *tourist*

U

último *last* (final)

ultramarinos (m) *grocer*

un/una *a*

uña (f) *finger nail*

único *single* (only)

universidad (f) *university*

uno *one*

urgente *urgent*

usar *to use*

uso (m) *use*

usted *you* (formal)

utensilios de cocina (m pl) *cooking utensils*

útil *useful*

uvas (f pl) *grapes*

V

vacaciones (f pl) *holiday*

vacío *empty*

vacuna (f) *vaccination*

vagón (m) *carriage* (train); el vagón-restaurante *restaurant car*

vainilla (f) *vanilla*

vale *OK*

valle (m) *valley*

válvula (f) *valve*

vapor (m) *steam, steamer* (boat); al vapor *steamed*

vaqueros (m pl) *jeans*

varios *several*

vaso (m) *glass* (for drinking)

váter (m) *toilet* (item in bathroom)

¡váyase! *go away!*

veces: a veces *sometimes*

vegetariano *vegetarian*

vehículo (m) *vehicle*

veinte *twenty*

vela (f) *sailing; candle*

velocidad (f) *speed*

venda (f) *bandage*

vender *to sell*

veneno (m) *poison*

venir *to vome*; ¡venga aquí! *come here!*

ventana (f) *window*

ventas (f pl) *sales*

ventilador (m) *fan* (ventilator)

ventisca (f) *blizzard*

ver *to see*; no veo *I can't see*

verdad *true*; es verdad

it's true; ¿verdad? *isn't that so?*
verde *green*
verdulería (f) *greengrocer's*
verdura (f) *vegetables*
verja (f) *gate*
vestido (m) *dress*
veterinario (m) *vet*
vez: de vez en cuando *occasionally*
viajar *to travel;* viajar en avión *fly (of person)*
viaje (m) *journey;* el viaje de novios *honeymoon*
vida (f) *life*
vídeo (m) *video (film);* el (aparato de) vídeo *video recorder*
videocámara (f) *camcorder*
vídeo-juegos (m pl) *computer/video games*
viejo *old*
viento (m) *wind*
viernes *Friday*

vigilante nocturno (m) *night porter*
vinagre (m) *vinegar*
vinatero (m) *wine merchant*
vino (m) *wine*
violín (m) *violin*
visita (f) *visit;* las horas de visita *visiting hours;* la visita con guía *guided tour*
visitante (m/f) *visitor*
visitar *to visit*
visor de imagen (m) *viewfinder*
vista (f) *view*
vitaminas (f pl) *vitamin pills*
vivero (m) *garden centre*
vodka (m) *vodka*
volar *to fly* (plane, insect)
volver *to come/get back, return;* nos volvemos mañana *we get back tomorrow*
voz (f) *voice*
vuelo (m) *flight*

W, Y, Z

web site (f) *website*
whisky (m) *whisky*
y *and*
ya *already*
yo *I*
yogur (m) *yoghurt*
zanahoria (f) *carrot*
zapatería (f) *shoe shop*
zapatilla (f) *washing machine*
zapatillas (f pl) *slippers*
zapatos (m pl) *shoes;* los zapatos de deporte *trainers*
zona peatonal (f) *pedestrian zone*
zoo (m) *zoo*
zumo *juice* (m); el zumo de frutas *fruit juice;* el zumo de naranja *orange juice;* el zumo de tomate *tomato juice*

Acknowledgments

The publisher would like to thank the following for their help in the preparation of this book: Isa Palacios and Maria Serna for the organization of location photography in Spain; Restaurant Raymon at Mi Pueblo, Madrid; Magnet Showroom, Enfield, London; MyHotel, London; Peppermint Green Hairdressers, London; Coolhurst Tennis Club, London; Kathy Gammon; Juliette Meeus and Harry.

Language content for Dorling Kindersley by G-AND-W PUBLISHING
Managed by **Jane Wightwick**
Editing and additional input: **Cathy Gaulter-Carter, Teresa Cervera, Leila Gaafar**

Additional design assistance: **Lee Riches, Fehmi Cömert, Sally Geeve**
Additional editorial assistance: **Paul Docherty, Lynn Bresler**
Picture research: **Louise Thomas**

Picture credits

Key:
t=top; b=bottom; l=left; r=right; c=centre; A=above; B=below

p2 **Alamy:** *ImageState / Pictor International; p4/5* **Alamy RF:** *Image Source tl;* **Alamy:***D Hurst bl; Indiapicture bcl; p10/11* **Alamy RF:** *BananaStock cl; Getty: Taxi / James Day cbl;* **Ingram Image Library:** *bl; p12/13* **Alamy RF:** *Dynamics Graphics Group / Creatas cBr; John Foxx cAr; RubberBall br;* **DK Images:** *cl;* **Ingram Image Library:** *tl, cr; p14/15* **DK Images:** *tcr;* **Ingram Image Library:** *cl, cBl, cAr, cBr, bcr; p16/17* **Getty:** *Taxi / James Day bcr;* **Ingram Image Library:** *tr; p18/19* **DK Images:** *David Murray tr; p22/23* **DK Images:** *cl, Andy Crawford cAr; Susanna Price br; Magnus Rew tcrB;* **Ingram Image Library:** *tcr; p24/25* **DK Images:** *clA, Dave King tcr; p26/27* **Alamy RF:** *Dynamic Graphics Group / Creatas cl; p28/29* **DK Images:** *John Bulmer tcr; Dave King cr; Matthew Ward bclA;* **Ingram Image Library:** *bcrA, bcr; p30/31* **Alamy RF:** *Comstock Images bcl Think Stock bclA;* **DK Images:** *cl; p34/35* **Ingram Image Library:** *tcr; p36/37* **DK Images:** *bcl, bcr; Magnus Rew cl;* **Ingram Image Library:** *bl; p38/39* **Alamy RF:** *Imageshop / Zefa Visual Media cl;* **Ingram Image Library:** *cr; p40/41* **DK Images:** *Peter Wilson bl;* **Lee Riches:** *cl; p42/43* **Alamy RF:** *Image Source tcr, cAr, cAAr; p44/45* **Alamy:** *Jon Arnold Images br; ImageState / Ethel Davies bl; Vikki Martin cbl; Peter Titmuss bcrr;* **Alamy RF:** *Iain Davidson Photographic bcll; David O'Shea bcr; Courtesy of* **Renault:***c; p46/47* **Alamy RF:** *Imageshop / Zefa Visual Media br;* **Ingram Image Library:** *cr; Courtesy of* **Renault:** *tcrB;* **Lee Riches:** *bcl; p48/49* **Alamy:** *Balearic Pictures c;* **Alamy RF:** *Brand X Pictures bcl;* **DK Images:** *tcr, bcl; Neil Lukas bcr; John Miller crA;* **Lee Riches:** *bcl; p50/51* **Alamy:** *Peter Titmuss cr;* **Lee Riches:** *c; p52/53* **Alamy:** *Jean Dominique Dallet tcr;* **Alamy RF:** *Image Farm Inc cAr; Imageshop - Zefa Visual Media tcrB;* **DK Images:** *cl; p54/55* **Alamy:** *Jackson Smith cBl;* **Alamy RF:** *Brand X Pictures cl; John Foxx c; Image Source cAr; ThinkStock tcr;* **DK Images:** *Andy Crawford bcl; p56/57* **Alamy:** *Balearic Pictures clA;* **Alamy RF:** *Brand X Pictures clAA;* **DK Images:** *cl; Neil Lukas cl; John Miller tcll;* **Lee Riches:** *bc; Courtesy of* **Renault:** *bc; p58/59* **Alamy:** *Michael Juno tcr;* **Alamy RF:** *Brand X Pictures cBl, cBBl; Ingram Publishing cAAl;* **DK Images:** *cAl; Max Alexander cBr; p60/61* **Alamy:** *Robert Harding Picture Library bcr;* **Alamy RF:** *Image Source cAl;* **DK Images:** *Steve Gorton bl, tcrB; Dave King cr;* **Ingram Image Library:** *tcr; p62/63* **DK Images:** *Stephen Whitehorn c; p64/65* **Alamy:** *Arcaid bcrA; Mike Kipling c;* **Alamy RF:** *GKPhotography cBr; Goodshoot bcr; Justin Kase tcrB;* **DK Images:** *Steve Tanner cAr;* **Ingram Image Library:** *tcr; p66/67***Alamy:** *Arcaid tl;* **Alamy RF:** *Ingram Publishing cl;* **DK Images:** *tr; Stephen Whitehorn bl;* **Ingram Image Library:** *br; p68/69* **Alamy:** *Balearic Pictures cr; directphoto.org cAr; Doug Houghton cl; Indiapicture clB;* **Alamy RF:** *CoverSpot cBl;* **Lee Riches:** *cBr; p72/73* **Alamy RF:** *imagebroker tcrB;* **Image Source cAr; Comstock Images tcr;* **Avery Weight-Tronix:** *cl; p74/75* **Alamy RF:** *Doug Norman bl;* **Ingram Image Library:** *br; p76/77* **Alamy:** *Balearic Pictures cBl; Indiapicture bl;* **Alamy RF:** *Coverspot cBl; p78/79* **Alamy RF:** *Luca DiCecco bcl; Steve Hamblin br; p80/81* **Getty:** *Taxi / Rob Melnychuk bc;* **Ingram Image Library:** *cAr;* **Xerox Ltd.** *tcr; p82/83* **Alamy:** *wildphotos.com tcr;* **Alamy RF:** *FogStock cAAl; Momentum Creative Group cAl; Shoosh / Up the Res cBl;* **Ingram Image Library:** *cl; p84/85* **Alamy:** *Brand X Pictures cr; fl* **Alamy RF:** *BananaStock bl; Comstock Images c; SuperStock tr;* **Ingram Image Library:** *crB; p86/87* **Alamy RF:** *Luca DiCecco bcl;* **Getty:** *Taxi / Rob Melnychuk tc; p90/91* **Alamy RF:** *Brand X Pictures tcr;* **DK Images:** *cl; David Jordan cAr; Stephen Oliver cr;* **Ingram Image Library:** *cBr; p92/93* **Alamy RF:** *Pixland cr;* **DK Images:** *cl; Guy Ryecart tr; p94/95* **Alamy:** *David Kamm cl; Phototake Inc bcl;* **Alamy RF:** *Comstock Images cr; ImageState Royalty Free bcr;* **DK Images:** *Stephen Oliver tcr; p96/97* **Alamy RF:** *Pixland br;* **DK Images:** *tl;* **Ingram Image Library:** *cr; p98/99* **Alamy:** *Andrew Linscott c; Shotfile cr;* **Alamy RF:** *Bildagentur Franz Waldhaeusl bl; ThinkStock br; p100/101* **DK Images:** *Steve Gorton tcr; p102/103* **Alamy:** *Hortus b; D Hurst tcrB;* **Alamy RF:** *image100 tcr; br; Barry Mason cAAr;* **Ingram Image Library:** *cAr; p104/105* **DK Images:** *Paul Bricknell cl(6); Jane Burton bcl; Geoff Dann cl(2); Max Gibbs cl(4); Frank Greenaway cl(3); Dave King cl(1), clr; Tracy Morgan cl(5); p106/107* **Alamy:** *Shotfile cr;* **Alamy RF:** *Barry Mason br; p110/111* **Alamy RF:** *Think Stock cr;* **DK Images:** *Andy Crawford cl; bcrA; p112/113* **Alamy RF:** *Dynamic Graphics Group / Creatas tcr; image100 bl;* **Ingram Image Library:** *cl; bcrA; p114/115* **Alamy:** *John Cole cr;* **Alamy RF:** *Image Source cAr; Index Stock cAl; jackhollingsworth.com tcr; p116/117* **Alamy RF:** *Dynamics Graphics Group / Creatas clA; John Foxx clB; p118/119* **Alamy:** *D Hurst c;* **Alamy RF:** *Pixland tcr; p120/121* **Alamy:** *ImageState / Pictor International cl; Shotfile cBl;* **Alamy RF:** *Sarkis Images tcr;* **DK Images:** *bcl; p122/123* **Alamy RF:** *BananaStock cA;* **Ingram Image Library:** *cl; p124/125* **Alamy:** *ImageState / Pictor International bclA; Shotfile cBl;* **DK Images:** *bcl; Paul Bricknell tc(1); Geoff Dann tc(3); Max Gibbs tc(1); Frank Greenaway tc(2); Dave King tc(4); Tracy Morgan tc(5);* **Ingram Image Library:** *bl; p126/127* **Alamy:** *Jean Dominique Dallet clB;* **Alamy RF:** *Imageshop - Zefa Visual Media blA; Image Farm Inc bl; p128* **DK Images.**

All other images **Mike Good.**